BRADLEY
VS
BMP

Desert Storm 1991

MIKE GUARDIA

First published in Great Britain in 2016 by Osprey Publishing,
PO Box 883, Oxford, OX1 9PL, UK
1385 Broadway, 5th Floor, New York, NY 10018, USA
E-mail: info@ospreypublishing.com

Osprey Publishing, part of Bloomsbury Publishing Plc

A CIP catalog record for this book is available from the British Library

Print ISBN: 978 1 4728 1520 0
PDF ebook ISBN: 978 1 4728 1521 7
ePub ebook ISBN: 978 1 4728 1522 4

Index by Rob Munro
Typeset in ITC Conduit and Adobe Garamond
Maps by bounford.com
Originated by PDQ Media, Bungay, UK
Printed in China through World Print Ltd.

16 17 18 19 20   10 9 8 7 6 5 4 3 2 1

Osprey Publishing supports the Woodland Trust, the UK's leading woodland
conservation charity. Between 2014 and 2018 our donations are being spent
on their Centenary Woods project in the UK.

www.ospreypublishing.com

Acknowledgments

Special thanks to the following individuals who graciously provided interviews
and photographs for inclusion in this book: Tim Tomlinson, Dave Feller,
Colonel (Ret.) Douglas Macgregor, Emil Bagalso, Bill Virrill, Chad King,
Mike Rhodes, Randy Trahan, Vladimir Ryabtsev, Matthew Lee, and Joe
Deskevich. Select quotations from Mike Guardia, *The Fires of Babylon*: *Eagle
Troop and the Battle of 73 Easting* (Havertown, PA: Casemate, 2015).
Reprinted with permission.

Editor's note

In this book, US customary measurements (yards, feet, inches, pounds,
ounces) are used, with the exception of gun calibers, armor thicknesses, and
horizontal distances; for these three, metric measurements are given with the
US customary equivalent in parentheses. For ease of comparison please use the
following conversion table:

1 mile = 1.6km
1yd = 0.91m
1ft = 0.30m
1in = 2.54cm/25.4mm
1lb = 0.45kg

Title-page photograph: A pair of ill-fated BMP-1s destroyed in the Euphrates
River Valley, March 1991. Despite its perceived strengths and supposed
resiliency, the BMP-1 would prove to be easy prey for almost any coalition
armored fighting vehicle that engaged it. (US Army)

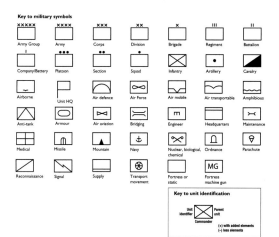

Key to military symbols

CONTENTS

INTRODUCTION

On the morning of August 2, 1990, more than 100,000 Iraqi troops and several hundred Iraqi armored fighting vehicles (AFVs) stormed across their country's south-eastern border into neighboring Kuwait. Encountering only piecemeal resistance, Iraqi tanks thundered into the heart of Kuwait City. A coordinated air–ground attack decimated the Dasman Palace, home to the Emir of Kuwait, Sheikh Jaber III al-Amhad al-Jaber al-Sabah. The emir himself and a few members of his staff barely escaped with their lives as they fled Kuwait by helicopter. The last transmission made over the state-run radio network was an appeal for help.

An Iraqi BMP-1 captured by US Marines during the Gulf War of 1991. The Soviet-built "Boyevaya Mashina Pekhoty" (BMP: Infantry Fighting Vehicle) was one of the most significant innovations in the history of mechanized warfare, enabling an infantry squad to ride into battle with the benefits of unprecedented mobility, firepower, and armored protection. With more than 55,000 examples built since 1966, the BMP has become one of the most widely produced AFVs in history. Within a decade of the BMP's arrival, NATO members had laid the groundwork for vehicles such as the British FV150 Warrior, the West German Marder, and the American M2/M3 Bradley. (US Department of Defense)

The stage was set for a confrontation between the Iraqi armed forces and an international coalition led by the United States and determined to protect neighboring Saudi Arabia and liberate Kuwait. Iraq's brutal dictator, Saddam Hussein, was certain that his armed forces – the fourth largest in the world and equipped with large quantities of sophisticated Soviet armor – would make short work of any rescue force that came to liberate Kuwait. He wagered that the Americans would lead a military response against Iraq but that, as he famously quipped, America was "a society that cannot accept 10,000 dead in one battle." He was confident that after the Americans had suffered a few thousand casualties, they would sue for peace on Iraq's terms.

At the forefront of the US and Iraqi forces that would clash in the Persian Gulf were the US M2 Bradley and the Soviet-designed BMP-1 – rival infantry fighting vehicle (IFV) designs that had never previously encountered one another in combat. While American and Soviet military technology played important roles in many conflicts in the Middle East and Southeast Asia, no data had been collected on the comparative use of the two powers' IFVs. This was due to the fact that American-backed forces such as the Israelis and the South Vietnamese had no IFVs at the time. The closest comparable US vehicle was the M113 armored personnel carrier (APC), which fulfilled the role of a "battlefield taxi" and occasional reconnaissance vehicle. Meanwhile, the Soviet-backed armies of the Arab world were making extensive use of the BMP-1 – albeit with varying degrees of success.

As the Cold War between the superpowers waned, however, the US-led effort to liberate Kuwait would provide Western analysts with an opportunity to compare American and Soviet IFVs directly. Now, the untested M2 Bradley would make its combat debut against the Soviet-built BMP-1, nearly 20 years its senior.

Washington, DC, June 7, 1991: an M2A0 Bradley in the victory parade following Operation *Desert Storm*. Delivered in 1983 after more than a decade in development, the M2 Bradley IFV and M3 Bradley Cavalry Fighting Vehicle (CFV) offered a remarkable improvement over the M113 APC. At the forefront of the coalition advance would be the 2d Armored Cavalry Regiment (ACR), its 2d Squadron newly equipped with the M2A2 Bradley. (Photo by Visions of America/UIG via Getty Images)

CHRONOLOGY

1954
The BTR-50P APC enters Soviet service.

1958
The Schützenpanzer 12-3 IFV enters West German service.

1959
BMP development begins.

1961
Field trials of BMP prototypes begin.

1962
The M113 APC is first fielded by US forces in Vietnam.

1964
The US Mechanized Infantry Combat Vehicle (MICV-65) program begins.

1966
Limited production of the BMP begins.

1968
Development of the US Armored Reconnaissance Scout Vehicle (ARSV) begins.

1969
The BMP is delivered to the Soviet Army.

1973
The US MICV-65 program is canceled amid budget cuts and a public backlash against the Vietnam War.
The BMP-1 debuts in combat during the Yom Kippur War.
The Iraqi Army receives the BMP-1.

1974
The US ARSV program is canceled.

A 1991 aerial photo depicting the charred remains of an Iraqi BMP-1 (left) and a Type 69 main battle tank (right). Both vehicles likely belonged to a Republican Guard battle group, all of which were organized in a similar manner to the latter-day Soviet armored formations. (US Department of Defense)

Eagle 34, an M2A2 Bradley, delivers Iraqi POWs to the rear echelon of the 2d ACR's area. Many Bradleys served this function as they could carry more enemy prisoners than an M1A1 Abrams main battle tank. (Bill Virrill)

1978

The US Department of Defense accepts the XM723 prototype for the US Army's new IFV program.

1980

The Iran–Iraq War begins.
The Soviet Union unveils the BMP-2.

1983

The first Bradley IFVs and CFVs are delivered to the US Army.

1986

The US Army unveils the upgraded M2A1/M3A1 Bradley.
The BMP-2 is first delivered to Iraq in limited numbers.

1988

The Iran–Iraq War ends.
The US Army unveils the upgraded M2A2/M3A2 Bradley.

1990

August 2: Iraq invades Kuwait.

1991

January 15: Saddam Hussein ignores a United Nations (UN) deadline to withdraw from Kuwait; US-led coalition begins air campaign against Iraq.
February 24: The official start of the coalition ground war against Iraq.
February 26, 1500hrs: The 2d ACR meets elements of the 3rd *Tawakalna ala-Allah* Mechanized Division at the battle of 73 Easting.
February 28, 0800hrs: Ceasefire.

DESIGN AND DEVELOPMENT

BMP

ORIGINS

In many ways the arrival of the BMP in the 1960s was surprising, because the Soviet Army had been slow to mechanize its infantry forces. During World War II, the Red Army did not field significant numbers of AFVs. Instead, Soviet defense planners concentrated on manufacturing tanks and assault guns, leaving the infantry to rely on their feet and whatever wheeled vehicles they could muster. While Soviet forces were victorious on the Eastern Front, the lack of mechanized infantry was a major shortcoming of the Red Army's fighting power.

The Soviets themselves seemed to recognize this deficiency and began mechanizing their infantry forces in the late 1940s. They briefly experimented with half-track configurations (including the American M3, which the Soviets received under Lend-Lease, and examples of the SdKfz 251 captured from German forces) but promptly abandoned them. "The half-track approach," according to historian Steven J. Zaloga, "was not as popular as it combined the complexity and cost of tracked vehicles but lacked the superior mobility of fully-tracked vehicles. This was not a unique viewpoint – half-track suspensions were almost universally abandoned after 1945 in favor of wheeled or tracked configurations" (Zaloga 1994: 4). Thus, the Soviets' first attempt to mechanize their infantry divisions came with the fielding of the rather unsatisfactory BTR-152, which had virtually no cross-country capabilities and performed only marginally well on improved roads.

Since mechanized infantry units were expected to keep pace with their armored counterparts, the Soviet Army began soliciting designs for a tracked infantry transport. Ideally, Soviet commanders wanted an infantry transport that could travel at speeds of up to 45km/h (28mph) offroad and 60km/h (37mph) on improved level surfaces. The vehicle also needed an operational range in excess of 300km (186 miles). These performance metrics would enable the infantry carrier to match the mobility of the T-62 and T-64 main battle tanks. The first of these designs was the BTR-50P, developed in 1951 by the Kotin Design Bureau in Leningrad. It was little more than an adaptation of the PT-76 light tank, but was nonetheless a significant step forward in developing a tracked IFV. To fulfill its role as an infantry vehicle, the BTR-50P removed the PT-76's turret and gave the entire chassis an open-air top with seating for two infantry squads (20 dismounts in total). The BTR-50P was a mobile and resilient vehicle, but it was poorly configured for its role as an infantry transport. For instance, a soldier had to climb over the sides to enter and exit the vehicle – a cumbersome process that could be fatal in combat. Also, the seating for 20 dismounts was not conducive to proper personnel management. Since the Soviet rifle companies were triadic (three platoons of three squads each), commanders had to mix squads from different platoons in the same vehicle. As a result, Soviet designers soon realized that their infantry vehicles had to be tailored to squad size.

While recognizing the need for a squad-sized infantry vehicle, the Soviet Army also began revising its tactical doctrines. By the late 1950s, strategists within NATO and the Warsaw Pact saw the future of warfare dominated by tactical nuclear weapons. As a result, conventional ground forces could no longer operate in massed formations; they would have to operate in a dispersed fashion using highly mobile combined-arms teams to present a smaller target for the enemy. For Soviet defense planners, the doctrine shifted: could conventional infantry survive on a nuclear battlefront? All the

This BTR-50 in East German service is pictured in Berlin during May 1973. The BTR-50P entered Soviet service in 1954 and equipped the motorized rifle regiments of Soviet and East German armored divisions and mechanized brigades; Egypt, Syria and others used the vehicle in the Six-Day War (1967) and the Yom Kippur War (1973). (Photo by Probst/ullstein bild via Getty Images)

evidence indicated the answer to be "No," and thus the IFV concept was born. Since delivering dismounted troops to a nuclear battlefield would expose them to radiation, the solution was to have the infantry squad fight from *inside* an armored vehicle when operating in a contaminated environment, or dismount and fight conventionally when the threat of nuclear weapons wasn't present.

Even so, the West Germans beat the Soviets to the punch. In 1958 a revolutionary AFV appeared in West German service – the Schützenpanzer 12-3, arguably the world's first IFV. West German doctrine favored an AFV that allowed mechanized infantry to fight alongside the tanks, rather than simply ferrying them to the edge of the battlefield in the manner typified by contemporary American AFVs such as the M75 and M59. Armed with a 20mm autocannon housed in a small turret, the SPz 12-3 carried five troops – half a squad – as well as its three-man crew. Importantly, however, the West German vehicle's five dismounts could use their personal weapons from their mount only after emerging from the roof hatches to fire, thereby exposing themselves to enemy fire and the use of chemical weapons.

When the Main Administration of the Armored Force (GBTU) issued its BMP requirement in the late 1950s, the Soviet Army specified that the platform should have a special armament based on a one-man turret. The main weapon, subsequently, was the new 73mm 2A28 Grom (Russian for "thunder") semiautomatic gun that was fed by an autoloader. This developmental 73mm gun was a revolutionary design and very similar to the shoulder-fired rocket-propelled grenade (RPG). The gun's primary ammunition would be the 73mm PG-15 rocket projectile. The PG-15 was similar to the older SPG-9 rocket, but with a much greater range to accommodate the standoff distances associated with armored warfare. Other militaries (on both sides of the Iron Curtain) had experimented with rocket launchers and recoilless rifles mounted atop their armored vehicles, but most refused to mount such weapons in the turret because of the gas blowback following the projectile's discharge. To correct that problem, early designs of the 2A28 gun featured a bore evacuator that served as a "release valve," of sorts, whenever the Grom was fired.

Alongside the Grom, the Soviet Army specified a coaxial machine gun with a caliber of no less than 7.62mm. To that end, the Tula Design Bureau selected the 7.62×54mmR PKT machine gun, which had become a mainstay of Soviet armored vehicles including the T-62 main battle tank and the BRDM-2 amphibious armored scout car. To give the vehicle an antitank capability, designers simply added a rail-launcher for the 9M14 Malyutka antitank missile (NATO reporting name: AT-3A "Sagger A"), which entered service in 1963.

Although the Soviet Army specified the BMP's armament package in advance, the chassis design had been left open for debate. For instance, the question remained as to whether the BMP would be a tracked vehicle, a wheeled vehicle, or a hybrid that retained qualities of both. Most agreed that a fully tracked vehicle would be the most versatile, but the Soviet Army's leadership was hesitant given the level of maintenance and the complexity of the system itself. Indeed, many believed that the maintenance requirements for a tracked system would be beyond the capabilities of the rank-and-file conscript mechanics. The deadlock over the wheeled-versus-tracked platform led the GBTU to announce a design competition in which four prominent design bureaus would submit prototypes for field testing.

TOWARD THE BMP-1

The competing bureaus included the automotive plants in Bryansk and Rubtsovsk, along with the Isakov Konstruktorskoye Buro (KB = Design Bureau) in Chelyabinsk and the Gavalov KB in Volgograd (which later produced the BMD-1 Airborne Assault Vehicle). The Bryansk Automotive Plant's design was known as the Obyekt 1200 – an 8×8 wheeled configuration that looked remarkably similar to the BTR-60/70/80 series of vehicles. The Rubtsovsk plant entered the competition with a most unusual design. Their Obyekt 19, as it was called, was a mix of wheels and tracks and featured four road wheels similar in configuration to the BRDM-2. However, between the two wheels on either side of the vehicle, there lay a retractable track assembly that could be lowered to improve mobility across rough terrain not suitable for wheeled vehicles. Obyekt 19's engine was rear-mounted and the crew (including dismounts) entered and exited the vehicle through hatches on the roof. The Gavalov KB submitted two designs that, at first glance, were remarkably similar: the Obyekt 911 and Obyekt 914. The 911 had a fully tracked chassis, yet underneath the vehicle's hull were four retractable road wheels which, theoretically, could be lowered to increase the vehicle's speed on appropriate terrain. The 914 shared most of the design features found on the 911, except for the retractable wheels. The Isakov design, Obyekt 765, was a conservative tracked platform with a front-mounted engine and rear-mounted troop compartment.

Field trials began in 1961 at the Soviet Army proving grounds in Rzhev and Kubinka. Obyekt 1200 performed well given that it was a solely wheeled platform. However, the 1200's results reflected the same mobility limitations as those of the BTR-series vehicles. Obyekt 19 and Obyekt 911 – each with their hybrid track-wheel configurations – performed poorly and were quickly eliminated from the stakes. Obyekt 914, despite its impressive performance during the field trials, could not

Pictured here is a BMP-1, the most-produced variant of the BMP, on static display at Bolling Air Force Base, Washington, DC. (US Department of Defense)

11

recover from the perceived design flaws of a rear-mounted engine and roof hatches being the only means of egress. Accordingly, Soviet military planners saw the rear-mounted engine as a space thief – space that could be better utilized for accommodating dismounted troops. In addition, the roof-mounted hatches did not facilitate a rapid egress from the vehicle. In the end, Obyekt 765 won the competition. In many ways, the rear troop compartment was the deciding factor, since the 914 and 765 had similar performance metrics. After Obyekt 765 was accepted as the official BMP, limited production began in 1966. Following further operational trials (and a few redesigns of the original 765 chassis), the BMP was fully accepted into Soviet service in 1969.

From the time Obyekt 765 debuted in 1966 until it was delivered as the official BMP in 1969, there were at least four prototype production runs, each one an improvement in design and functionality on the previous. For instance, Soviet Army evaluators noticed that the BMP had a serious weight imbalance caused by the location of the engine and transmission. Furthermore, when trying to negotiate water obstacles, the BMP's hull tended to porpoise along the waterline. Thus, to add additional buoyancy, designers added a 10in hull extension. This feature became standard on the BMP-1, which itself emerged as the "definitive version" of the BMP in 1970. The BMP's new swimming air intake featured a snorkel to prevent water from flooding the engine.

IMPROVING THE BMP

Throughout its service life, the BMP-1 has been modified into different variants and undergone several upgrades. Modifications to the original BMP-1 included Soviet-built variants for reconnaissance (BRM and BRM-1K), command and control (BMP-1K and BMP-1Ksh), artillery target acquisition (PRP-3 and PRP-4), ammunition resupply, armored recovery (BREM-2 and BREM-4), and combat-engineer support (IRM); Warsaw Pact and other countries developed yet more variants.

An important upgrade to the BMP series of vehicle came in 1974, in the wake of the Yom Kippur War of October 1973, in which the Arab-operated BMP-1s had not performed as well as expected. Postwar analyses revealed, for instance, that the one-man turret configuration reduced the crew's situational awareness and placed an undue burden on the vehicle commander, who did not have the same field of vision as that of his elevated gunner. Furthermore, the BMP-1's 9M14 Malyutka antitank missile could not be guided effectively from the confines of the one-man turret. Ergonomics aside, the BMP-1's 73mm main gun was highly inaccurate beyond 500m (545yd) and the vehicle's armored skin was vulnerable to .50-caliber ammunition. To make matters worse, the crew had to keep some of the vehicle hatches open to prevent the vehicle from overheating. This not only compromised the safety of the crew, but made the BMP-1 vulnerable to small-arms fire from higher ground. Nevertheless, Arab crews praised the vehicle for its speed, agility, and low profile.

Motivated by these after-action reports, Soviet designers unveiled the BMP-1P as a stopgap measure to address some of the more serious design flaws. For instance, smoke-grenade launchers were installed toward the rear of the turret and the manually guided 9M14 Malyutka missile system was replaced with the semiautomatically guided 9K11 Fagot system (NATO reporting name: AT-4 "Spigot"). The 9P135 launcher was fitted to the turret roof, but this positioning compelled the gunner to expose himself to enemy fire before launching the missile.

Shortly thereafter, the design team at the Kurganmashzavod factory unveiled their prototype for the BMP-2, code-named Obyekt 675. The design featured the BMP-1 hull but with a two-man turret, accommodating the gunner and commander.

A Bulgarian BMP-1P during the St. George Parade in 2009. Weighing 14.8 tons, the BMP-1P retained the 73mm main gun and powerplant of the BMP-1, but replaced the 9M14 Malyutka (AT-3A "Sagger-A") missile system with the 9M113 Konkurs (AT-5 "Spandrel") missile system and featured an additional firing port. The BMP-1P replaced the BMP-1 in production from 1979. (KGG1951/CC-BY-3.0)

BMP-1 SPECIFICATIONS

Crew: Two (driver, gunner)

Dismounts: Nine (including commander)

Combat weight: 15.3 tons

Length: 22ft 1in

Width: 9ft 8in

Height: 6ft 4in

Armament

Main gun: 73mm 2A28 Grom smoothbore semiautomatic
  gun

Main gun rate of fire: 7–8rds/min

Main gun elevation: +33° / -4°

Gunner's sight: 1PN22M1 (6× / 6.7×)

Commander's sight: TKN-3B (4.2× / 5×)

Coaxial machine gun: 7.62×54mmR PKT

Main gun ammunition: 40

Machine-gun ammunition: 2,000

Missile: 9M14M Malyutka-M

Missile stowage: One ready, four stowed

Motive power

Engine type: UTD-20 six-cylinder four-stroke diesel

Horsepower: 300hp

Power-to-weight ratio: 19.6hp/t

Fuel capacity: 122 US gallons

Performance

Ground pressure: 8.9psi

Max road speed: 65km/h (40mph)

Max cross-country speed: 45km/h (28mph)

Max water speed: 8.0km/h (5.0mph)

Max range (roads): 600km (375 miles)

Fuel consumption: 0.38 US gallons per mile

Gradient: 35° (25° side slopes)

Vertical obstacle: 2ft 4in

Trench crossing: 8ft 2in

Ground clearance: 1ft 3in

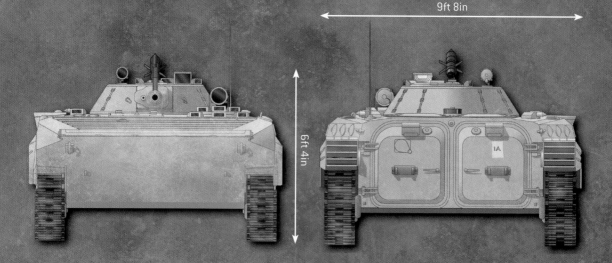

BMP-1, 3rd *TAWAKALNA ALA-ALLAH* MECHANIZED DIVISION, FEBRUARY 1991

In the BMP-1, the eight dismounts of the infantry squad were seated back-to-back, facing outward in the rear of the vehicle. Each infantryman had his own firing port and periscope from which he could engage enemy targets without exposing himself to enemy fire or a nuclear-contaminated battlefield. The crew compartment (housing the driver, gunner, and squad leader) was protected by a PAZ nuclear over-pressurization and filtration system. The one-man turret, meanwhile, was situated in front of the crew compartment and slightly to the right. The driver sat in the front-left of the vehicle with the squad leader seated behind him and off to one side of the turret. The soldiers could enter or exit the vehicle through the rear roof hatches or the two rear doors.

Initially painted in Soviet dark green, the Iraqi BMP-1s were overpainted in various shades of sand color, which faded and discolored in the harsh environmental conditions. The Republican Guard had a variety of markings for their T-72s and BMP-1s. The BMP-1s of the 3rd *Tawakalna ala-Allah* Mechanized Division were identified by the yellow flashes painted on their sides and their rear hatches. Each flash was stenciled with the parent brigade's designation in Arabic numerals.

22ft 1in

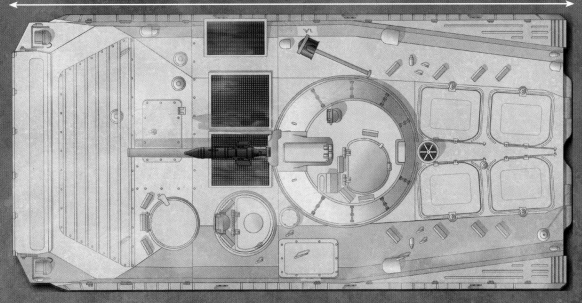

A destroyed Iraqi BMP-2K command vehicle, pictured in April 2003 during Operation *Iraqi Freedom*. The BMP-2's 30mm 2A42 autocannon was selected for a number of reasons. First, the BMP-1's 73mm semiautomatic gun had been rendered obsolete with the development of Chobham reactive armor, first implemented on the M1 Abrams tank. Although the 30mm autocannon couldn't penetrate tank armor, it still had significant anti-helicopter capabilities. Second, the 2A42 had a longer maximum effective range – nearly 4,000m (4,375yd). This allowed the BMP-2 to engage enemy vehicles from standoff ranges and better support its tank counterparts. As with the BMP-1, the BMP-2's gunner could engage targets during low visibility with the use of a night sight and an infrared searchlight. The vehicle commander, meanwhile, had a periscopic day sight and an active infrared night sight. Third, the 2A42 had a higher maximum elevation, which allowed the gunner to engage enemy dismounts on higher ground. Like the BMP-1, the BMP-2 found a wide export market to the usual Soviet clientele. Although 200 BMP-2s were purchased by Saddam Hussein in 1986, the BMP-1 remained the primary variant in Iraqi service in early 1991. Most of the BMP-2s in Iraqi service would be destroyed during Operation *Desert Storm*, but a few remained in service by the time Operation *Iraqi Freedom* began in 2003. Since that time, the remaining Iraqi BMP-2s have been scrapped. (US Marine Corps)

The 73mm Grom semiautomatic gun aboard the BMP-1 was replaced by the 30mm Shipunov 2A42 autocannon. Unlike the Grom, the Shipunov has two selectable rates of fire: a slow rate of up 300rds/min, and a fast rate of up to 550rds/min. Two ammunition trays near the turret floor carry 160 Armor-Piercing (AP) rounds and 340 High Explosive (HE) rounds. Two types of AP rounds are carried: the Armor-Piercing with Tracer (APT) has a muzzle velocity of 970m/sec (3,182ft/sec) and can penetrate up to 20mm of armor, while the Armor-Piercing Discarding Sabot with Tracer (APDS-T) has a muzzle velocity of 1,120m/sec (3,675ft/sec) and can penetrate armor up to 25mm thick. Taken together, these firepower metrics give the BMP-2 enough stopping power to halt an M2 Bradley and many other IFVs of the NATO contingent. The APT round, however, will not penetrate the upgraded armor of the M2A3 Bradley, which was specifically designed to defeat the 2A42 autocannon. Unlike the 73mm Grom, the 2A42 has an advanced stabilization system that gives the gun better accuracy while the vehicle is moving; and it can be aimed and fired by either the gunner or the squad leader (who doubles as the vehicle commander). Meanwhile, to retain the BMP's antitank capabilities, Soviet designers improved its guided-missile armaments. Now, the BMP gunner could operate a 9P135M launcher (accommodating up to three different types of antitank missiles) safely from the confines of his vehicle.

Delivered to the Soviet Army in 1987, and unveiled to the public in 1990, the BMP-3 outclasses most second-generation main battle tanks (1960–80). It did not appear on the battlefields of Kuwait and Iraq in 1991, however. To date, the BMP-3 has only seen combat with Russian forces in Chechnya and with United Arab Emirates forces during the Yemeni Civil War; it has also been exported to Venezuela.

BRADLEY

ORIGINS

Decades before the Bradley debuted with American ground forces, the closest thing the US Army had to an IFV was the M113 APC. As its name implied, it was little more than a "battlefield taxi" – a vehicle whose sole purpose was to deliver troops to the front lines where they would fight dismounted. The M113, though reliable, did not offer much in the way of protection or stealth. It was 8ft 2.5in tall, weighed 13.6 tons, and had a six-cylinder diesel engine which was incredibly loud, and a chassis protected by aluminum armor with a maximum thickness of 38mm. The intention was to protect the occupants from small-arms fire while making the vehicle light enough to be air transportable and amphibious.

When the M113 first appeared in 1959, the US military (like most of its NATO allies) was shifting its focus away from conventional ground forces in favor of nuclear weapons. According to most military analysts, tactical nuclear weapons would play a more significant role on the modern battlefield than would conventional troops. Since fighting in contaminated environments seemed to be a foregone conclusion, US policymakers wrestled with the problem of how to protect their troops from radiation. To that end, the Army began looking for an APC that would allow infantrymen to fight from within the vehicle if the battlefield were tainted by nuclear fallout.

Beginning in 1964, the Army accepted bids for such a vehicle. The program was called the "Mechanized Infantry Combat Vehicle – 1965," or MICV-65, and the

A BMP-3 during rehearsals for the 2008 Moscow May Day Parade. This revolutionary design features an improved chassis with a rear-mounted V-6 engine, but still allows room for up to nine dismounts to sit in the rear. The armament consists of a 100mm 2A20 rifled main gun alongside a 30mm 2A72 autocannon, along with the standard 7.62x54mmR PKT coaxial machine gun. The 2A20's autoloader holds 22 rounds of ZOF17 and ZOF32 projectiles. The BMP-3 also has an antitank missile system that fires the 9M117 Bastion laser-guided missile (NATO reporting name: AT-10 "Stabber"); six are carried. Unlike the BMP-1 and BMP-2, however, the BMP-3's missile launcher is integrated inside the turret, no longer mounted externally and thereby exposing the crewman to enemy fire. (Vladimir Ryabtsev)

An M113 Armored Cavalry Vehicle (ACAV) in Vietnam, 1966. The US Army's experience in Vietnam underscored the need for an IFV instead of a "battlefield taxi." The M113 was vulnerable to enemy mines and anti-armor tactics, and not well suited for armored combat. Crucially, it lacked any weapon that could penetrate tank armor at normal combat ranges. Its primary armament was a .50-caliber machine gun; and a dismounted infantryman riding in the back had to expose himself through the roof hatch to engage the enemy. One expedient solution to this problem was the M113 ACAV, which was nothing more than an M113 with armor slats placed around the roof hatches to protect dismounts from small-arms fire. (US Army)

initial design incorporated elements of the M109 Paladin self-propelled howitzer. However, the Army concluded that it was too heavy to serve as an IFV and too slow to keep pace with the forthcoming MBT-70 tank (which would later evolve into the M1 Abrams). The Army would undoubtedly have made more headway on the MICV-65 had it not been for the Vietnam War. Indeed, as the US military sent more of its forces to Southeast Asia, programs like MICV-65 were placed on the back burner.

By 1968, as the war in Vietnam dragged on, the Army reopened the MICV program amid reports of the M113's lackluster performance and news of the Soviet BMP. Over the next five years, the Army evaluated several prototypes for the MICV. Nearly all were rejected as being too slow, too heavy, or inadequately armored. Congress then canceled the program amid the backlash against the war in Vietnam.

At around the same time, however, the Army launched a program for a new armored reconnaissance vehicle. Billed as the Armored Reconnaissance Scout Vehicle (ARSV) program, it sought a platform to replace the M113 Armored Cavalry Vehicle (ACAV) and the M551 Sheridan light tank, which first saw combat in Vietnam in 1969. With a steel turret and aluminum hull, the M551 proved to be highly vulnerable to anti-armor rockets and mines. The prototype vehicle for the ARSV program (called the XM800-T) was an impressive design, but post-Vietnam budget cuts led to the program's cancellation in November 1974. However, military analysts soon realized that the MICV and ARSV could be combined into a single platform. After all, partisan

politics did not negate the Army's need for a stronger IFV – during Vietnam, the Soviet armored vehicles had jumped a generation ahead of their Western counterparts. Indeed, while the Americans were still relying on the M48/M60 tanks and the M113 series, the Soviet Army had fielded the T-64 and T-72 main battle tanks and the latest versions of the BMP.

But before the Army committed to building its own IFV, it examined a number of foreign-built vehicles to see if they would be a better fit. The French AMX-10 was evaluated but quickly dropped from the stakes. The West German Marder, however, was very popular among US Army officers stationed in West Germany. Army evaluators were impressed, too, but they ultimately rejected the vehicle due its high cost, light armor, and lack of amphibious capabilities. Ideally, the American IFV would need to be able to protect the crew from 14.5mm cannon-fire and carry a main gun with a stabilized system that would allow it to fire on the move. Yet the most glaring concern would be how to reconcile firepower and protection against mobility and stealth. Larger armaments and heavier armor would slow the vehicle down and increase the lifetime maintenance costs – both of which were undesirable for an American IFV. By nature, the IFV would have to be sufficiently agile to accommodate the rapid deployment needs of the infantry, yet offer its crew adequate protection from the normal variety of sidearms and shoulder-fired weapons.

The M113 was widely exported and many adaptations and developments of the type have appeared since its combat debut in 1962. Here, Iraqi soldiers in celebratory mood ride atop an M577 command vehicle captured from Iranian forces during the Iran–Iraq War. (Photo by François Lochon/The LIFE Images Collection/Getty Images)

The experimental XM723 IFV is offloaded from the cargo bay of a McDonnell Douglas YC-15 during loading/unloading trials in 1977. (US Department of Defense)

TOWARD THE BRADLEY

The initial prototype, designated the XM723, was developed by the FMC Corporation in 1973. It weighed 21 tons, had spaced aluminum armor that could withstand 14.5mm gunfire, and could accommodate 11 crewmen (commander, gunner, and driver – plus eight infantry). Unlike the M113, the XM723 had firing ports for the on-board riflemen, who sat facing the outside walls, rather than the center of the vehicle. Its most innovative feature, however, was a one-man turret with a 20mm autocannon. As with the BMP-1, the vehicle commander sat inside the hull.

Developed in 1976, the scout reconnaissance variant of the XM723 replaced the one-man turret with a two-man turret which featured a 25mm Bushmaster autocannon and a TOW (Tube-launched, Optically tracked, Wire-guided) missile launcher. The two-man turret, although taking up more space within the vehicle and thereby reducing the number of personnel who could be carried, gave the commander a better situational view of the battlefield. The TOW missiles gave the vehicle a strong anti-armor capability and would help it achieve parity with the Soviets' 9M14 Malyutka and 9K11 Fagot missile systems.

By 1978, the two-man turret design had been selected as the better of the XM723 variants. Thus, the two-man turret design (with its TOW missiles and 25mm main gun) became the standard-bearer for the IFV and the armored reconnaissance vehicle.

After the US Secretary of Defense, Harold Brown, gave his approval for production in early 1980 the vehicles were subsequently classified as the M2 Infantry Fighting Vehicle (IFV) and the M3 Cavalry Fighting Vehicle (CFV). The M3 CFV was nearly identical to the M2 variant; but instead of holding six infantrymen, it was configured to hold two cavalry dismounts. The additional space made available by the reduction in the number of dismounts accommodated extra TOW missiles, 25mm ammunition, and 84mm M136 CT4 shoulder-fired missiles. The firing ports were sealed on the M3 CFV as they were deemed non-essential to the cavalry missions.

As per recent tradition, the Army chose to the name the vehicle after a famous soldier. Originally, there were plans to name the M2 after General Omar N. Bradley and the M3 after General Jacob L. Devers, but the Army chose instead to name both vehicles after Bradley as the M2 and M3 were essentially the same design.

An M2A0 Bradley fires its 25mm M242 Bushmaster autocannon during Exercise *Shadow Hawk* *'87*. Prior to its deployment in the Gulf War, the Bradley had seen extensive service participating in arid-climate training scenarios. (US Department of Defense)

BRADLEY VARIANTS

Both the M2 and M3 received upgrades and led to successive variants over the years. In 1986, the Army unveiled the M2A1, in which space was made available for a seventh infantryman directly behind the turret. The M2A1 included an improved BGM-71D TOW-2 missile system, a Gas Particulate Filter System – for the vehicle commander, gunner, and driver only – and a Halon fire-suppression system. (The

M2A2 BRADLEY SPECIFICATIONS

Crew: Three (commander, driver, gunner)

Dismounts: Six

Combat weight: 33.6 tons

Length: 21ft 6in

Width: 10ft 9in

Height: 9ft 9in

Armament

Main gun: 25×137mm M242 Bushmaster chain-driven autocannon

Main gun rate of fire: 200rds/min

Main gun elevation: plus 57° / minus 9°

Gunner's sight: Raytheon ISU (4× / 12×)

Commander's sight: Via optical relay

Coaxial machine gun: 7.62×51mm M240C

Main gun ammunition: 300 ready, 600 stowed

Machine-gun ammunition: 2,200

Missile: BGM-71D TOW-2

Missile stowage: Two ready, five stowed

Motive power

Engine type: Cummins VTA-903T eight-cylinder four-stroke diesel

Horsepower: 600hp

Power to weight ratio: 17.9hp/t

Fuel capacity: 175 US gallons

Performance

Ground pressure: 10.5psi

Max road speed: 56km/h (35mph)

Max cross-country speed: 48km/h (30mph)

Max water speed: 6.4km/h (4.0mph)

Max range (roads): 400km (250 miles)

Fuel consumption: 0.7 US gallons per mile

Gradient: 60° (40° side slope)

Vertical obstacle: 3ft

Trench crossing: 8ft 4in

Ground clearance: 1ft 3in

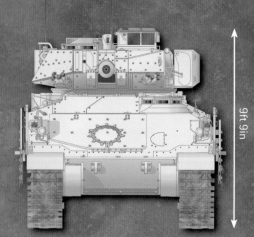

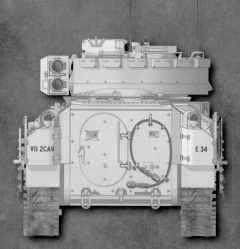

10ft 9in

9ft 9in

M2A2 BRADLEY, 2d SQUADRON, 2d ACR, FEBRUARY 1991

Like the BMP-1 and Marder, the Bradley had a front-mounted engine and a rear-mounted troop compartment. The driver was positioned on the left, just below the turret, and operated the vehicle with a hydrostatic steering system. Behind the driver was a "tunnel" leading to the rear crew compartment. Two of the dismounts sat back-to-back in this tunnel while the rest of the squad sat in the rear seating compartment proper. The two squad members in the tunnel operated the two left-side firing ports. The rear seating compartment was configured to seat two men to the right-side firing ports, and two men to the rear-door firing ports. The rear area also contained additional storage for 25mm ammunition (for the M242 Bushmaster autocannon) and extra TOW missiles. The turret of the Bradley sat off-center to the right, and held the vehicle commander and the gunner. The vehicle commander had 360° turret-mounted

periscopes and either he or the gunner could employ the Bushmaster autocannon.

For their deployment to Southwest Asia, US ground forces repainted most of their combat vehicles from Forest Green or the common NATO-pattern camouflage to CARC (chemical agent resistant coating) Tan 686. When the 2d ACR's tanks and Bradleys arrived in Saudi Arabia, they were hastily moved through "paint tents" in which each vehicle received its CARC Tan 686 scheme. The Bradleys in 2d Squadron, 2d ACR had no special insignia other than their vehicle number and unit identifiers stenciled on the rear. For example, this Bradley reads "E34" on the right (indicating that it is the 4th vehicle of 3d Platoon, Eagle Troop) and "VII 2CAV" on the left (indicating that the 2d ACR is part of VII Corps). The external stowage has been omitted from these illustrations to show details of the armor.

21ft 6in

An M3A2 Bradley demonstrates use of the BGM-71D TOW-2 missile at a gunnery range in West Germany. Although it provides the Bradley with a substantial antitank capability, the TOW missile can only be fired while the vehicle is stationary. Furthermore, the Bradley gunner has to guide the missile to its target via a complex and sensitive tracking system that requires a keen eye and a steady hand. (US Department of Defense)

original M2 and M3 had no integral chemical defense system, compelling the crew to wear nuclear, biological, and chemical (NBC) protective gear.) The M3A1 featured similar changes, but with all five of its crewmen benefiting from the Gas Particulate Filter System.

In 1988, the M2A2 arrived, with an upgraded armor package that better protected the vehicle against 30mm AP rounds (such as those fired by the BMP-2's 2A42 autocannon) and RPGs. Spaced laminate armor was installed on the hull rear and spaced laminate track skirts protected the track system and lower hull. More storage space was added to the turret and Kevlar spall liners were added to critical areas of the vehicle. The seating and stowage arrangements were also revised, with the dismount capacity becoming six once again. Although the first 662 production M2A2s had the original 500-horsepower engine, subsequent vehicles were fitted with an improved 600-horsepower engine in order to maintain performance. Gross weight increased to 33.6 tons as a result of these modifications. The M3A2 featured much the same upgrades as the M2A2, but moved the two cavalry dismounts to the left side of the vehicle to enhance their safety.

TECHNICAL SPECIFICATIONS

An understanding of the operational environment is central to any assessment of how the BMP-1 and Bradley performed during the Gulf War. In the harsh deserts of Iraq and Kuwait, the blistering heat could reach temperatures in excess of 110° Fahrenheit during the day, yet drop to near-freezing at night. The extreme differences in temperature each presented their own challenges. For instance, working in the daytime meant that soldiers had to rehydrate constantly. During the night, however, soldiers had to keep their gear dry, so as not to have anything freeze overnight. Although the Iraqis were accustomed to fighting in the arid climate, they too still needed to alleviate the effects of the heat. Iraqi commanders did not place a high emphasis on hygiene and nourishment, thereby inevitably degrading their soldiers' ability to fight, but many vehicle crews were allowed to keep vehicle hatches open during combat to prevent overheating. The downside of this, of course, was that it exposed the Iraqi crewmen to American indirect fire (particularly from mortars).

As brutal as these desert temperatures could be, however, the skies were often clear throughout the day. It rained very little in the desert, but sandstorms could become hurricanes in their own right. Although not deadly in themselves, sandstorms could send fine grains of sand into the most unthinkable places within a vehicle. Soldiers often remarked how tiresome it was to clean out sand from the vehicles' on-board instruments and engine blocks. To make matters worse, sandstorms could reduce visibility to zero, halting troop movements for hours on end. The Americans had the advantage with their superior combat optics, however, which allowed them to see and engage targets during the worst sandstorms while the Iraqis were blinded and disoriented.

The wreckage of an Iraqi BMP-1 after multiple direct hits. Although the BMP-1 had a larger-caliber main gun than the M2/M3 Bradley, the Soviet-designed weapon was notoriously inaccurate at ranges beyond 500m (545yd). (US Army)

The terrain was generally flat and featureless, which (on a clear day) gave virtually unrestricted visibility for nearly 5km (3 miles) in any direction. This open space allowed mechanized formations to spread their firepower over a wider area. It also facilitated better situational awareness for commanders. By the same token, however, these desert plains had no prominent landmarks upon which a soldier could orient his movement. Thus, it was easy to get lost in the desert. (The lack of landmarks is why some Gulf War battles were named for their gridline position on a military map.)

Although the terrain was generally flat, there were sand dunes and ridges that could present problems; a rise of even a few meters is significant as it can become an "intervisibility" line – meaning that an enemy vehicle could hide beneath the drop in elevation and an advancing vehicle might not detect the other until it was too late.

ARMAMENT

BMP-1

The BMP-1's most potent antitank weapon is its guided missile. Early versions of the BMP-1 carried the 9M14 Malyutka, which was fired from atop a 9S415 launch-rail system fitted above the main-gun tube. The Malyutka is known as a "manual command to line of sight" weapon and it bears some similarities to the TOW missile system later used on the American M2 Bradley. Upon firing the missile, the gunner has to track and steer the projectile by use of a joystick controller. The process of guiding the missile to its target requires extensive practice and dexterity, however, especially when trying to do so under the stress of combat – as the Arab forces had found during the 1973 Yom Kippur War. Because the missile climbs immediately after being launched, it takes time for its course to be corrected; this means its minimum range is around 700m (765yd). It takes about 30 seconds for the missile to reach its maximum range of about 3km (2 miles), giving the intended target time to take evasive action.

These shortcomings led Soviet designers to replace the Malyutka and its successor, the 9M14M Malyutka-M (NATO reporting name: AT-3B "Sagger B") with the 9K11

BMP-1 AMMUNITION

The 9M14M Malyutka-M missile (**1**) weighs 24lb overall, with the warhead accounting for 5.7lb. It travels at 115m/sec (377ft/sec), spinning at 8.5 revolutions per second. Four missiles are carried internally – two in the turret and two in the hull space – on the gunner's right-hand side.

A modified version of the projectile fired by the 73mm SPG-9 Kopye (Russian for "spear") recoilless gun, the PG-15V High Explosive AntiTank (HEAT) round (**2**) weighs 7.7lb. It has a muzzle velocity of 400m/sec (1,312ft/sec) – rising to 700m/sec (2,297ft/sec) after the rocket motor starts, some 10–20m (33–66ft) from the muzzle – and a maximum range of 1,300m (1,420yd). The PG-15V has a level trajectory out to 800m (875yd) but is very sensitive to crosswinds, making its accuracy more problematic. Although it is credited with an effective range of 700m (765yd), experience has shown that the round is notoriously inaccurate beyond 500m (545yd).

The PG-15V's warhead is hexagonal in shape, weighing 0.7lb but with the power to penetrate up to 350mm of steel. Based on these performance metrics, the BMP-1 could penetrate the frontal armor on any Western tank of the 1970s – including the US M48 and M60, the British Chieftain, and the West German Leopard 1. For later-generation tanks such as the US M1 Abrams, the French Leclerc, the British Challenger 1 and 2, and the West German Leopard 2, it could not penetrate the frontal armor, but could pierce certain areas of the side armor.

Designed for use against enemy dismounts, thinly armored vehicles, and field fortifications, the OG-15V (**3**) is a High Explosive Fragmentation (HE-Frag) round weighing 10.1lb. It has a muzzle velocity of 290m/sec (951ft/sec) and a maximum effective indirect-fire range against formation targets of 4,400m (4,815yd); against small point targets the effective direct-fire range is about 1,000m (1,095yd). It has a 1.6lb bursting charge, which gives the round a much greater blast effect than the PG-15V.

1 2 3

A close-up view of the BMP-1's primary armament. The BMP-1 featured a one-man turret, armed with a 73mm 2A28 Grom main gun. It also had an anti-armor punch in the form of the 9M14 Malyutka missile. (Darkone/CC-BY-SA-2.0)

Fagot and 9M113 Konkurs (NATO reporting name: AT-5 "Spandrel") on the BMP-1P from 1979 onward. Known as a "semiautomatic command to line of sight" weapon, the wire-guided Fagot entered Soviet service in 1970; the Konkurs entered service in 1974. The two missiles share the 9P135 launcher, mounted on the roof of the BMP-1. The Fagot has a 50 percent higher hit probability than the Malyutka and a more sophisticated guidance system that automatically corrects the missile's trajectory – thus eliminating the need for the joystick operator system. The Konkurs has an operational range of up to 4,000m (4,375yd) and a top speed of 200m/sec (656ft/sec).

At shorter ranges, the main armament aboard the BMP-1 is the 73mm 2A28 Grom semiautomatic gun, a smoothbore weapon initially serviced by an autoloader carrying 40 rounds of ammunition from a storage compartment on the right side of the turret floor. When the Grom debuted as the BMP-1's primary armament, the PG-15V was the only round available for the gun, but from 1974 the Soviets introduced the OG-15V projectile. Inside the turret, the gunner has a selector switch which allows him to choose the type of round to be loaded into the gun breech.

Designed to save time and manpower, the Grom gun's autoloader gives a rate of fire of 6–8 rounds per minute; but it also has a rather serious design flaw: like most Soviet main-gun autoloaders, the Grom's barrel has to be lowered in order to chamber the next round into the breech. This costs the gunner precious time as he has to re-acquire the target after each shot. Also, the Grom easily jams and its moving parts can frequently snag loose-fitting uniforms. When the BMP-1 was exported, several of the recipient armies – including the Iraqis – dismantled the autoloader as the PG-15V and OG-15V rounds could easily be loaded by hand. Although this created more work for the gunner, many BMP-1 crews found that they could load the rounds faster by loading them manually.

The Grom gun has a 70 percent hit probability against a tank from a distance of 500m (545yd). At 800m (875yd) against the same target, however, the hit probability decreases to 50 percent. The Grom's performance is even worse while the BMP-1 is moving because the gun is not stabilized. The Grom proved unequal to the task of operating in the rugged terrain of Afghanistan, as although it can be elevated to +33°, aimed fire is only possible up to +15°.

The 7.62×54mmR PKT coaxial machine gun is one of the many variants of the PK general purpose machine gun in Soviet service from the early 1960s. With an effective range of 1,500m (1,615yd), it has a theoretical rate of fire of 700–800rds/min, although 250rds/min is more realistic in combat conditions. Up to 2,000 rounds of machine-gun ammunition are carried on-board the BMP-1. As well as the coaxial PKT, the BMP-1 could project a lot of close-range firepower from its eight infantry dismounts; one was the squad machine-gunner, typically armed with a 7.62x54mmR PKM light machine gun, who occupied the forward-most firing port, while the other dismounts carried variants of the 7.62×39mm AK-47 or AKM assault rifle. Finally, perhaps one in two BMP-1s in Soviet service carried a man-portable air defense missile such as the 9M32 Strela 2 (NATO reporting name: SA-7 "Grail").

M2A2

The deadliest weapon aboard the M2A2 Bradley was the twin-mounted BGM-71D TOW-2 antitank missile system. The TOW missile was initially developed by Hughes Aircraft in the 1960s under the designation "XBGM-71A" and was designed for both ground and aerial platforms. Introduced into US Army service nearly 50 years ago, the TOW missile remains in service with the US Army and the militaries of more than 40 nations. Aside from the Bradley, the TOW missile has been integrated into thousands of stationary, vehicular, and aerial platforms worldwide.

The TOW missile has an operational range of more than 4,000m (4,375yd), making it the Bradley's farthest-reaching weapon. Of the Bradley's armament, the TOW missile is the only weapon capable of destroying an enemy tank. The Bradley's twin TOW missiles are housed in a special rectangular compartment situated on the left side of the turret. This launching compartment is fully retractable and can only be reloaded manually. Furthermore, because the TOW missile's instrumentation is so sensitive, and the system itself is wire-guided, it can only be fired when the vehicle is stationary. Herein lies what many Bradley crews have perceived to be the vehicle's greatest liabilities. If engaged in a firefight, the crew must risk the life of the junior-ranking dismounted soldier by having him exit the Bradley, jump on the top deck of the vehicle, and manually insert the missile tubes into their launchers while being exposed to enemy small-arms and – even worse – main-gun fire. Additionally, stopping the vehicle in order to fire the TOW missile forfeits the biggest advantage the Bradley has on the modern battlefield: its speed. When the vehicle halts, it naturally becomes an easier target for an enemy vehicle. Finally, Bradley crews have often complained that the TOW missile is not a "fire-and-forget" system. The TOW operator does not have the luxury of simply aiming the reticle, acquiring a target, and then firing the missile before searching for another target. On the contrary, the TOW operator must maintain his focus on the target he intends to destroy and guide his missile all the way to the target. Only after he confirms that it has been destroyed can he search the battlespace for another target.

The Bradley is also armed with a 25×137mm M242 Bushmaster autocannon, capable of destroying lightly armored vehicles, low-flying aircraft, and most field fortifications. Weighing 242.5lb with a 6ft 8in-long barrel, the Bushmaster is an electrically powered, chain-driven, automatic cannon fed by a link belt with dual ammunition capabilities that allow the crew to select between AP and HE rounds. The dual-feed ammunition system has a system of sprockets and extractor grooves to control how the rounds are fed into the receiver. The M242 Bushmaster can fire several types of 25mm ammunition, including the M791 APDS-T round and the M792 HEI-T round.

A close-up of the Bradley's primary armament, shown here on an M2A0. The 25mm M242 Bushmaster is an autocannon that fires four types of ammunition. It can shoot farther (and at a higher rate of fire) than the BMP-1's 73mm 2A28 Grom semiautomatic gun. For anti-armor capabilities, the twin-mounted TOW missiles can destroy any main battle tank at ranges of up to 4,000m (4,375yd). (US Army)

The M242 has three selectable rates of fire: Single Shot, Low Rate, and High Rate. In Single Shot mode (as the name implies), the gunner or commander can only fire one round at a time. Either man must release the trigger after every shot if he wishes to fire another round. In Low Rate mode, the gunner or commander can fire approximately 100rds/min. In High Rate mode, the gunner or commander can fire nearly 200rds/min. However, for either Low Rate or High Rate modes of fire, gunners are recommended to engage targets with no more than 10–15-round bursts at a time. This method of engagement helps prevent the barrel from overheating and prematurely "cooking off" a round.

The secondary armament aboard the Bradley is the 7.62×51mm M240C coaxial machine gun. The C-variant of the M240 distinguishes it as a vehicle-mounted gun; it differs from its infantry counterpart in that it uses a right-handed feed and employs a charging cable instead of a charging handle. The trigger well has also been removed to facilitate the gun being fired by a solenoid. The M240C has a rate of fire of 750–950rds/ min and can do so at velocities of 853m/sec (2,799ft/sec). Its maximum effective range is 3,725m (4,075yd). As with the Bushmaster, gunners are encouraged to engage targets with short bursts (5–10 rounds) to prevent the barrel from overheating.

An adaptation of the M16 assault rifle, the 5.56×45mm M231 Firing Port Weapon is configured to fire only on automatic and has special tracer rounds to help the shooter aim and adjust his fire. Since the infantryman can only aim the M231 via a periscope, the tracer round is critical to attaining accurate fire. The four ports on the sides of the M2 IFV were removed for the M2A2 and subsequent variants, leaving only the two in the ramp.

PROTECTION

BMP-1

The BMP had little in the way of armored protection. Its outer body consisted of welded, rolled steel that was, at most, only 33mm thick. The distribution of armor

BRADLEY AMMUNITION

As the acronym "TOW" (Tube-launched, Optically Tracked, Wire-guided) implies, the BGM-71D TOW-2 missile (**1**) is launched via a tube and optically tracked via the gunsight as it leaves the housing group. The launch motor (or "booster") ejects the missile from the tube, at which point four forward wings indexed at 45° spring open, while four tail control surfaces flip open toward the rear. Once the projectile leaves the tube, it travels at more than 300m/sec (984ft/sec). Propulsion is sustained by the flight motor which fires through lateral nozzles. As the missile flies through the air, the gunner uses the joystick on his instrument panel to make slight corrections to the missile's trajectory as it hurtles toward the target. These path corrections are sent digitally from the instrument panel via the wire attached to the end of the missile. This wire is coiled behind the missile in the launch tube and unravels as the missile travels farther away from the launch tube.

The primary ammunition types used by the Bradley's 25mm M242 Bushmaster autocannon during the Gulf War were the M791 and M792. The M791 (**2**) is designated an "Armor-Piercing Discarding Sabot with Tracer," or APDS-T, and is capable of penetrating most lightly armored vehicles, self-propelled artillery, and low-flying aircraft. The round itself consists of a tungsten-alloy penetrator, pressed-in tracer pellets, an aluminum windshield, a staked aluminum base, a welded nylon nose-cap, and a molded discarding-type nylon sabot. Both the nose-cap and sabot are discarded as soon as the bullet leaves the barrel. The remaining projectile is spin-stabilized and destroys the intended target via kinetic energy. The M791 has a velocity of 1,345m/sec (4,413ft/sec) and a maximum effective range of 2,000m (2,190yd) due to the tracer burnout, although the projectile will remain accurate up to 2,200m (2,405yd). During Operation *Desert Storm*, the M791 APDS-T was highly effective in destroying enemy BMP-1s, BRDMs, and MT-LBs.

The M792 (**3**) is an incendiary round, officially termed "High-Explosive Incendiary with Tracer," or HEI-T, and can destroy unarmored vehicles and low-flying aircraft. It can also destroy enemy fortifications and suppress troops that are beyond the range of the Bradley's coaxial machine gun. Like its APDS-T counterpart, the M792 is a fixed-type, percussion-primed round. The steel-case projectile contains an M758 mechanical fuse, 1.1oz of high explosive mix, and a pressed-in tracer. The M792 travels at a maximum speed of 1,100m/sec (3,609ft/sec). Upon impact, the M758 fuse ignites; the resulting explosion casts fragments from the steel body of the projectile over a 16ft radius. With a maximum effective range of 3,000m (3,280yd), the M792 HEI-T is unique in that it has three different ways of detonating: direct impact, grazing impact, and self-destruct. Direct impact, as the name implies, means that the round explodes upon impact with another object. The grazing impact feature allows the round to detonate if any part of the projectile (along its trajectory) grazes the surface of a target. The self-destruct feature allows the projectile to detonate automatically at a range of 3,000m if it has not hit a target by that point.

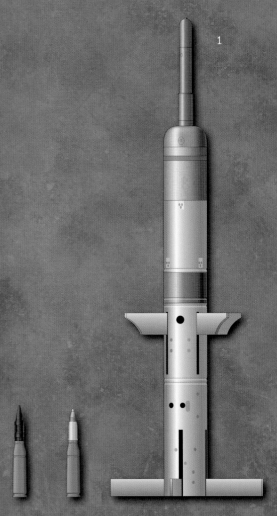

1

2   3

An Iraqi BMP-1 destroyed by the 2d Brigade, 3d Armored Division on the evening of February 26, 1991. (Dave Feller)

was intended to protect the BMP-1 during a frontal advance; consequently the side armor was especially thin, making the vehicle vulnerable to fire from heavy machine guns at close range. In the wake of the Soviet invasion of Afghanistan in 1979, the BMP-1's 16mm hull-side armor was increased by 10mm, resulting in the BMP-1D. The Iraqis sought to add appliqué armor to some of their BMP-1s in the months before the 1991 Gulf War conflict, but few of the vehicles received this upgrade in time for the campaign.

The space inside the BMP-1 was very restricted, prompting the occupants to stow their gear outside the vehicle while on combat operations; as well as blocking the entry hatches, this sometimes impeded use of the BMP-1's armament. Even with gear stowed outside the vehicle, the cramped internal layout of the BMP-1 presented a significant risk to the occupants, in that a well-placed hit could ignite the closely placed ammunition and fuel tanks and cause an explosion, killing all the dismounts. The meager protection afforded by the BMP-1 led many rifle squads to ride on the top of the vehicle when not actually in combat. The Iraqis, among other clients of the Soviet Union, reduced the number of men in their rifle squads owing to the lack of space inside the BMP-1.

To protect against NBC contamination, the BMP-1 could be hermetically sealed by locking all the hatches; it had an air filtration system and a device that could detect radioactive and chemical agents, as well as chemical decontamination kits. Although early production examples of the BMP-1 did not carry smoke-grenade launchers, the vehicle had a built-in smoke emitter that could create smoke for concealment by injecting fuel onto the engine manifold.

M2A2

As speed, stealth, and mobility are the Bradley's greatest assets, the light-armored skin allows the vehicle to fulfill its battlefield role. The Bradley's exterior armor is composed of a high-laminate 7000-series aluminum/zinc alloy. Although lightweight, this alloy gives the Bradley sufficient protection against enemy small-arms and 30mm main-gun fire. Even so, this aluminum armor raised serious questions about the Bradley's survivability in combat. There was an additional concern regarding the storage of large quantities of ammunition within the vehicle's hull; for if the vehicle were hit by a large main-gun round, or a perfectly aimed RPG, the resulting penetration might ignite the stored ammunition and turn the vehicle into a catastrophic kill.

Here, an M3A0 is shown. Externally, all M3 variants of the Bradley are virtually identical to their M2 counterparts. Although the Bradley is, by definition, a lightly armored vehicle, its heaviest armor lies in the front of the vehicle. Successive variants, beginning with the M2A2 and M3A2, featured additional slat armor that boosted vehicle protection. This appliqué armor has the added benefit of being "explosive-reactive," meaning that it is designed to detonate upon impact from a large-caliber projectile. This means that the resulting outward explosion deflects the projectile and negates its penetrative capabilities. Even on the upgraded variants, however, the Bradley's hull is perhaps the weakest part of the vehicle, as it consists of a 7107 Aluminum alloy. During the Gulf War of 1991 and Operation *Iraqi Freedom* from 2003, many Bradley crews resorted to lining the vehicle floor with sandbags as a safeguard against landmines, though many of these crewmen admitted that this countermeasure would not have done much to protect them. (Emil Bagalso)

To address these issues, the US Department of Defense introduced spaced laminate belts and heavy-duty steel skirts to the side of the M2A2 and M3A2. Although this improved these vehicles' overall armored protection, the additional armor also increased the overall weight to 33.6 tons and necessitated the deletion of four of the six firing ports (see above). However, during combat operations in the Persian Gulf and Operation *Iraqi Freedom*, these armor add-ons did not significantly degrade the Bradley's performance.

Although the original M2/M3 Bradley had no integral chemical defense system, the M2A1 incorporated a Gas Particulate Filter System for the commander, driver, and gunner. All variants carried two four-barreled smoke-grenade launchers on the turret front, which could be used to launch chaff and flares as well as smoke for concealment.

MOBILITY

BMP-1

The BMP-1 is powered by a UTD-20 six-cylinder, four-stroke diesel engine, located in the hull front center, which provides 300 horsepower. The fuel tanks have a combined capacity of 122 US gallons; the manual transmission has one reverse and five forward gears. The BMP-1 has its drive sprockets at the front, with six road wheels on each side, and a torsion-bar suspension system. The prototype BMP featured a new track design that was very similar to that of the T-64 main battle tank. Since the BMP was expected to keep pace with armored formations, speed was of the essence. To facilitate ease of driving, Soviet designers gave the BMP a driving yoke steering system – a radical departure from the traditional "clutch-and-brake" lever system found on almost every Soviet armored vehicle at the time. The BMP-1 has a top road speed of 65km/h (40mph) and an operational range of 600km (375 miles).

Two US Marines lower the trim vane on the front of an Iraqi BMP-1, February 1991. The trim vane was a mechanism that improved the BMP's stability when conducting amphibious operations. Soviet designers had intended the BMP to be fully amphibious, but the proposed hydro-jet system was dropped in favor of an advanced track-propulsion system that put the vehicle on a par with Western APCs of similar size and weight. Although the BMP retained a few amphibious qualities, e.g. its high-depth tolerance in fording operations, it was never truly an amphibious vehicle in the sense of the PT-76 light tank or the BRDM-2 amphibious armored scout car. (US Marine Corps)

M2A2

The Bradley's propulsion is accomplished via a VTA-903T eight-cylinder, four-stroke diesel engine which provides 600 horsepower. The fuel tanks have a combined capacity of 175 US gallons. The vehicle's HMPT-500 hydro-mechanical transmission from Combat Propulsion Systems provides three speeds forward and one in reverse. The Bradley's drive sprockets are located at the front, with six individually sprung road wheels on either side. Like most armored vehicles in the US inventory, the Bradley has a torsion-bar suspension system. The suspension rests firmly over six separated road wheels on either side of the vehicle. The tracks, made of steel with detachable rubber pads, are 21in wide and have a ground contact length of 12ft 10in. The M2A2 Bradley has a hydrostatic steering system with a steering yoke. The vehicle has a top speed of 56km/h (35mph) and an operational range of 400km (250 miles).

An M2A2 Bradley leads a convoy across a pontoon bridge into Bosnia on December 31, 1995 as part of Operation *Joint Endeavor* — one iteration of NATO's many peacekeeping missions in the Balkans. During Operation *Desert Storm* in 1991, several M2A2s were equipped with the TRIMPACK Global Positioning System (GPS), a technology that was still in its infancy at that time. (US Army)

THE STRATEGIC SITUATION

Iraq's invasion of Kuwait on August 2, 1990 took the world by surprise. Saddam Hussein had never been well-liked in the international community, but his unprovoked aggression against Kuwait shocked even his staunchest critics. For many, the thought of a full-scale invasion – with tanks and mechanized divisions – seemed anachronistic. News outlets around the world seemed to be asking the same question: "What was Saddam thinking?"

Saddam Hussein rose to power in the 1970s following the Ba'ath Party revolution. As he ascended to the presidency, Saddam ruled Iraq with a degree of brutality

An M2A0 Bradley prepares for action, 1991. On paper, the inaugural forces of Operation *Desert Shield* were woefully outnumbered and outgunned by the Iraqis. For example, the 101st Airborne Division (Air Assault) was a light infantry force equipped with airmobile assets. In the 82d Airborne Division, the heaviest weapon on the ground was the M551 Sheridan light tank. The 24th Infantry Division (Mechanized), XVIII Airborne Corps' only heavy asset, was equipped with advanced American armored vehicles – including the M1 Abrams, M2/M3 Bradley, and the M270 Multiple Launch Rocket System (MLRS) – but even it could not match the Iraqi armored divisions "tank-for-tank" in a contest of numbers. Therefore, it seemed that these early coalition forces would be little more than a speed bump if Iraqi aggression spilled into Saudi Arabia. (US Army)

An M2A2 Bradley IFV proudly displays the American flag in the deserts of Iraq, 1991. Aside from sporting its national colors, this Bradley shows how adaptive the US mechanized troops were at stowing gear aboard their vehicles. Since the inside of the Bradley was cramped and marginally ventilated, Bradley crews (including dismounts) strapped their field bags and other personal items to the side of the vehicle. For the most part, these items remained on the vehicle during combat operations - provided they weren't hit by shrapnel or enemy bullets. The front slope of the vehicle also served as a handy storage rack, accommodating concertina wire and even collapsible bed cots. (TM 6741-F5, The Tank Museum)

reminiscent of Hitler and Stalin. Nevertheless, he seemed poised for a long and prosperous rule of Iraq until his fortunes changed in the wake of the Iranian Revolution in 1979. Fearful that Ayatollah Khomeini's rhetoric would galvanize Iraq's Shiite majority, Saddam preemptively invaded Iran on October 22, 1980. The ensuing Iran–Iraq War lasted eight years and ended in a bloody stalemate that claimed more than 300,000 Iraqi dead. Aside from the untold cost in human suffering, the conflict left Saddam burdened with a multi-billion-dollar war debt, most of which had been financed by Kuwait. But rather than pay his debt to the Kuwaiti government, the "Butcher of Baghdad" simply invaded his neighbor to the south. To justify the invasion, Saddam reignited the long-standing border dispute between the two countries. He also made false allegations that the Kuwaitis had been slant-drilling Iraqi oil and that they were deliberately trying to keep the price of oil low by producing more than OPEC's set quotas. Kuwait held 10 percent of the world's oil reserves and generated 97 billion barrels of crude each year. Thus, Saddam reasoned that if he could not repay his debt, he would simply annex the tiny emirate and take over its petroleum industry.

Following the subsequent Iraqi invasion of Kuwait, what truly shocked the international community was the sheer barbarity of the Iraqi Army. At times, it seemed that Iraqi soldiers were torturing Kuwaitis simply for their own amusement. The United Nations responded by issuing their normal variety of condemnations. Undeterred by the rhetoric, the Iraqi dictator massed his forces along the Saudi Arabian border and dared the world to stop him. Economic and military sanctions soon followed, and President George H.W. Bush authorized the first US military deployments to the region.

A US M1A1 Abrams tank in the Saudi desert, February 12, 1991. Deployed alongside the M2/M3 Bradley, the M1A1 Abrams was arguably the most advanced tank in the world. Nevertheless, like the Bradley, it remained untested in combat. The first contingent of Abrams tanks arrived in Saudi Arabia as part of the US 24th Infantry Division (Mechanized) in September 1990. Armed with a 120mm main gun and equipped with laser rangefinders and an advanced "shoot on the move" stabilization system, the Abrams was far superior to any tank in Saddam Hussein's arsenal. Throughout the Persian Gulf conflict, the M1A1 Abrams deployed as part of a true combined-arms team. In most instances, the M2/M3 Bradley scouted forward of the Abrams' positions as the American divisions advanced into Iraq. Once visual or direct-fire contact with the enemy had been made, the Bradley would hold the enemy before passing the fight to the Abrams. From there, the Abrams could either engage the enemy by itself or work with the Bradley in a "hunter-killer" team using a deadly combination of "see and shoot" tactics. Using the Bradley's superior optics, the Abrams crewmen could home in on enemy vehicles and destroy them with superior firepower. The Iraqi variant of the T-72 tank, known as the "Lion of Babylon," was an impressive machine on paper, with a high-velocity 125mm gun and higher top speeds than the Abrams, but these front-line Iraqi tanks were plagued by the same lackluster maintenance programs that pervaded Saddam's military. Additionally, the Iraqis' gunnery skills were inferior to those of their Allied counterparts. Thus, the M1A1 Abrams often made short work of T-72s on the front lines of Iraq. (Photo by Richard Ellis/Getty Images)

On August 6, 1990, elements of the US XVIII Airborne Corps received their orders to move to the Persian Gulf. This contingent included the 82d Airborne Division, 101st Airborne Division (Air Assault), and the 24th Infantry Division (Mechanized). Within days, the US Navy aircraft carriers USS *Saratoga* and USS *Dwight D. Eisenhower* were en route to the Persian Gulf while coalition air squadrons began pouring into Saudi Arabia. These initial deployments became known as Operation *Desert Shield* – a deterrent against Saddam Hussein lest he turned his forces on the Kingdom of Saud. According to historian Jeffrey Clarke of the US Army Center of Military History,

> The mission of DESERT SHIELD was to defend Saudi Arabia with whatever forces were on hand while a buildup of additional forces was occurring. Success relied in part on presenting the Iraqis the illusion of facing a more formidable force than the United States was initially able to bring into the country. Had the Iraqis attacked in force before the defenses were in place, the results could have been catastrophic. (US Army 2010: 16)

Historians have debated just how effective Operation *Desert Shield* could have been if the Iraqi Army had crossed the border into Saudi Arabia in August–September 1990. Luckily, no such attack ever came; but as summer turned to fall, Saddam refused to bow to international pressure. Thus, by November 1990, the political objectives of the US-led coalition had changed. With the blessing of the United Nations, President Bush committed the US military to liberate Kuwait. This new objective required an offensive action, but the current defense posture along the Saudi–Iraqi border would not permit it. In a televised address on November 9, 1990, President Bush announced that he was sending the US VII Corps into Saudi Arabia.

February 27, 1991: an AH-64A Apache helicopter, armed with AGM-114A Hellfire anti-tank missiles, is prepared for a mission during Operation *Desert Storm*. As per the doctrinal organization of the armored cavalry regiment, attack helicopters such as the AH-64 Apache and the AH-1 Cobra played a critical role in suppressing the enemy on the battlefield. In 1991 the 2d ACR had an entire squadron (4th Squadron) dedicated to attack aviation. At the battle of 73 Easting, the regiment's 4th Squadron was joined in its efforts by the 2d Battalion, 1st Aviation Regiment, detached from the 1st Armored Division. This combination of forces brought a deadly mix of aerial firepower to the front lines. While the AH-1 Cobra was a tried and true workhorse of the air cavalry, the AH-64 was a relative newcomer. Indeed, the Apache had made its combat debut barely a year prior to the Gulf War – during the invasion of Panama in 1989. During the battle of 73 Easting, Apaches destroyed targets in greater depth beyond the 2d ACR's limit of advance. These close air support strikes prevented some Republican Guard units from closing on Ghost Troop's position. (Photo by US Army/Getty Images)

While the United States, Britain, and France favored a direct attack on Iraq, their Arab coalition partners wished to concentrate on the liberation of Kuwait. The eventual plan was a result of extensive consultation and compromise:

> In the planned offensive, fighting would begin with a multi-phased air campaign to establish preconditions for ground assault. Coalition air forces would successively smash Iraqi air defenses, secure air supremacy, suppress Iraqi command and control, isolate the Kuwaiti Theater of Operations (KTO), and attrit enemy ground forces in the path of the proposed offensive. The ground assault would begin with a division-size feint up the Wadi al Batin and a supporting attack by the marines reinforced with an Army armored brigade through the elbow of Kuwait. Arab thrusts equivalent in size to that of the marines would go in on their left and right. A marine amphibious feint would tie Iraqi units into coastal defenses, while an air assault deep into Iraq would isolate the KTO from the Iraqi core around Baghdad. The main attack would be that of the VII Corps, consisting of five heavy divisions, four separate field artillery brigades, an armored cavalry regiment, and a separate aviation brigade. This massive armored thrust would envelop the Iraqi line at its far-west end before turning east to annihilate the Republican Guard and then sweep across the northern half of Kuwait. The four-division XVIII Airborne Corps would ride the VII Corps' left flank and continue to isolate the KTO from the west while assisting in closing the trap to the east. With the phased arrival of the VII Corps and the maturation of the plan of attack, the stage was set for Desert Shield to become Desert Storm. (US Army 2010: 28–29)

In the early-morning hours of January 15, 1991, coalition forces received the news that Saddam Hussein had missed his deadline to withdraw from Kuwait. In a televised speech, President Bush announced the start of a massive air campaign that would weaken the Iraqis' resistance ahead of the ground war. Operation *Desert Shield* had now become Operation *Desert Storm*.

After nearly five weeks of aerial bombardment, President Bush issued his final ultimatum on February 21: Saddam Hussein had 24 hours to withdraw his forces from Kuwait or face destruction at the hands of coalition ground forces. Despite this ultimatum, the Iraqi dictator dug in his heels and told his troops to prepare for combat. The following day, with the 2d Armored Cavalry Regiment (ACR) leading the way, VII Corps began its advance into Iraqi territory.

OPPOSITE VII Corps' dispositions at 2300hrs on February 23, 1991.

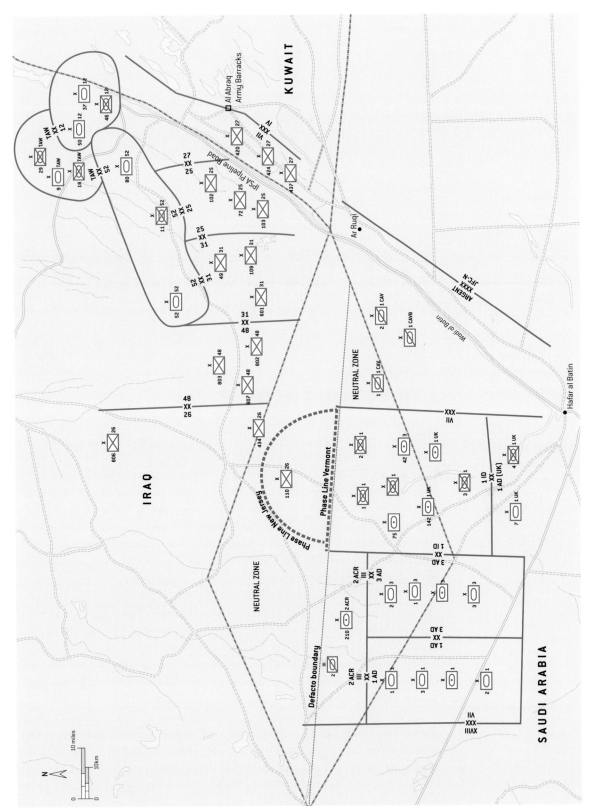

THE COMBATANTS

ETHOS AND TRAINING

IRAQI

Iraqi doctrine was influenced by Soviet tactical methods; and according to Soviet tacticians, the BMP could not be effective in a conventional armored fight. They believed that, in a conventional war, NATO ground forces would proliferate their antitank teams, to which the BMP would be dangerously vulnerable. Thus to find a role for the BMP, new tactics were devised. The BMP could operate freely whenever there was little to no enemy resistance, e.g. during the "breakout" phase of an offensive operation or when pursuing a disorganized enemy retreat. In the face of a stronger enemy, however, the BMP's role would be relegated to part of a "tank–infantry team." The first tier of this team would be a platoon of tanks, which could disrupt the enemy's front-line formations and absorb the brunt of their antitank forces. Advancing 200m (220yd) behind the tanks would be the dismounted infantry, ready to clear any remaining antitank teams or lingering enemy scouts. Finally, the BMPs would follow about 300–400m (330–440yd) behind the dismounts, providing mobile fire support for the tanks and infantry. After the tanks and infantry had subdued the enemy, the BMPs would move forward to pick up their dismounted comrades en route to the next objective.

In the 1970s, Saddam Hussein's Iraq, while still enjoying friendly relations with the United States, solicited the Soviet Union for the latest in armored and mechanized vehicles. Aside from importing the T-72 main battle tank, Saddam's generals took a keen interest in the IFV. Iraq initially imported about 200 BMP-1s in 1973. However, after the start of the Iran–Iraq War in 1980, Saddam solicited his Communist patron for more than 700 additional BMP-1s and a priority shipment of BMP-2s. Over the

The longest conventional war of the 20th century, the Iran–Iraq War (1980–88) provided Saddam Hussein's armed forces with extensive combat experience while fielding – and opposing – a variety of Soviet and other military technology. In this picture, released on October 1980, Iraqi soldiers stand in front of AFVs including two BMP-1s near Khorramshahr, Iran. (AFP/Getty Images)

ensuing decade, Saddam's arsenal of IFVs grew to include more than 1,500 BMP-1s and BMP-2s, combined.

Little is known about the Iraqis' BMP gunnery or tactical training programs prior to the Gulf War. However, the performance of Iraqi mechanized units during the Iran–Iraq War can provide some insight into crew-level proficiency. The root of the problem was the culture of Saddam's army. Unlike the US Army, which was an all-volunteer force, the Iraqi Army derived most of its manpower from conscripts, many of whom were poorly educated and barely literate before being drafted at gunpoint. The limited technical training available to these troops did not help the Iraqi Army's combat effectiveness once Operation *Desert Storm* began. Furthermore, the Iraqi Army's leadership was paralyzed at every echelon through fear of Saddam's brutality. Purges within the officer corps were frequent. Thus, no Iraqi commander wanted to take risks or seek meaningful reform.

The Iraqi way of war discouraged initiative and independent thinking, especially at the tactical level. Soldiers and young officers were expected to be automatons who did not act without explicit orders. In combat, Iraqi field commanders gave their units carefully scripted battle drills consisting of rehearsed tasks that did not depend on high levels of initiative. This authoritative command-and-control structure worked well against the Iranians, whose army was equally inept and mismanaged in the wake of the Shah of Iran's demise in 1979, but would be disastrous against a professional fighting force like the US Army – an organization that encouraged low-level initiative and independent thought.

During the Iran–Iraq War, Iraqi BMPs and tanks were used almost exclusively for infantry fire support. Providing this direct-fire support to the infantry is exactly what the BMP was designed to accomplish; but the Iraqi Army's tactics undercut the BMP's viability. In combat, volume of fire supplanted accuracy and, as a consequence, there was less emphasis on precision gunnery. By the latter years of the conflict, Iraqi mechanized units were fighting a defensive war, and dug many of their BMPs (and

other armored vehicles) into static positions. The Iraqis may have thought this prudent, but it essentially defeated the dual purposes of having an IFV: speed and mobility. Since the BMP bore the brunt of the direct-fire infantry support during the war with Iran, the 73mm gun tubes had abnormally high usage rates. This was problematic for two reasons: (1) Soviet gun tubes of every caliber were not built to last and (2) the Iraqi maintenance program was notorious for cutting corners. Thus, by 1991, many BMPs were thrust into battle with worn-out gun tubes, which would further undermine a BMP gunner's accuracy on the front lines. Despite these glaring deficiencies within the Iraqi mechanized forces, Saddam's army was still considered one of the most combat-capable forces in the Arab world.

AMERICAN

When comparing the crewmen of the Bradley to those of the BMP, there can be little doubt that the Bradley crew had superior training and took better care of their platforms. The first Bradleys were delivered stateside in 1983 to the 2d Armored Division at Fort Hood, Texas. The first Bradleys arrived in Europe with the 3d Infantry Division in Frankfurt, West Germany. Although the Bradley passed its operational trials without incident, the vehicle's reception among American troops was mixed. Soldiers praised it for its improved armaments, but they took issue with the Bradley's high profile – the M2/M3 stood higher than the M1 Abrams tank and nearly as high as the M60 tank. Nor were Bradley crews enthusiastic about the complexity of the TOW missile system and its sensitivity. These criticisms aside, however, many soldiers welcomed the Bradley as a marked improvement over the M113, which for years had been derisively labeled a "death trap."

Two Bradley CFVs from 2d Squadron, 4th Cavalry (24th Infantry Division) wait their turn on the firing range in Saudi Arabia, December 19, 1990. The example in the foreground appears to be an M3A1, while the vehicle behind it is an M3A0. The Bradley CFV differed only slightly from the Bradley IFV. For example, the firing ports were sealed and many of the rear seats were removed to accommodate extra ammunition and provide stowage for the 84mm M136 CT4 shoulder-fired missiles. Most armored cavalry units deployed to the Persian Gulf with CFVs. One notable exception, however, was the 2d Squadron of the 2d ACR, which rode into combat aboard the recently issued M2A2 Bradley. (US Army)

The Bradley's fighting compartment was manned by the vehicle commander and the gunner, both of whom spent the most time preparing for the Bradley's biannual gunnery exercises. Since the beginning of the 1980s, the US Army had undergone a renaissance of sorts. Higher recruiting standards, tougher retention standards, and a greater emphasis on the "train as you fight" methodology had created a new generation of soldiers who were proud of their profession, and were demonstrably the best at it. In military competitions across Europe, US Army tank and Bradley crews were consistently outperforming their NATO counterparts – something that had been unheard of during the post-Vietnam malaise of the 1970s.

Unlike the BMP, the Bradley had never seen combat prior to the Gulf War. Even though the US military had brief interludes in Grenada (1983) and Panama (1989), no Bradleys or Abrams tanks were deployed to those conflicts. By 1991, however, the Bradley did have extensive operational experience from the annual REFORGER (REturn of FORces to GERmany) exercises in West Germany and at the National Training Center at Fort Irwin, California. Under realistic field conditions (and pitted against a Soviet-style opposing force) the Bradley had performed its duties well and was gaining admiration from its infantry and scout crews.

At the time, training for cavalry scouts occurred at Fort Knox, Kentucky, then home to the US Army Armor School. After completing their initial training (One-Station Unit Training for enlisted soldiers and the Armor Officer Basic Course for commissioned officers), cavalry soldiers were assigned to military installations worldwide, where they continued honing their skills as part of the unit's training program. By the end of the 1980s, many of these units had computer-based simulators within full mock-ups of a Bradley turret. These simulators provided a realistic training platform that soldiers could use repeatedly, allowing them to sharpen their gunnery skills at a fraction of the cost of a live-fire range. Aside from these gunnery simulators, many facilities offered a version of the Simulator Network (SIMNET). SIMNET linked several Bradley mock-ups into a computer network in which crews could fight one another (or fight a programmed enemy scenario) in a giant video-game setting that allowed them to analyze their successes and shortcomings.

An M2A1 Bradley passes the wreckage of an Iraqi BMP-1. Like other armored fighting vehicles, the Bradley is equipped with several outlets to accommodate external stowage. Perhaps the most obvious examples are the fasteners for so-called "pioneer tools." Found on the upper sides of the vehicle, these external fasteners secure shovels, axes, and other items that assist in the maintaining the Bradley's operational abilities in a tactical environment. The rear stowage boxes located just below the taillights provide adequate storage for first-aid items among other pieces of equipment. On the rear of the turret, the mounted ammo racks provide a ready source of ammunition. (US Army)

Bradley and tank crews further sharpened their tactical skills on the desert plains of the National Training Center at Fort Irwin, California. Every month, armored and mechanized units rotated through the Mojave Desert to test their battlefield synergy against the home unit that was specifically trained to replicate a Soviet-style enemy. The Bradley crews based in Europe had a similar opportunity during the annual REFORGER exercises. Although the terrain of Western Europe lent itself to a different set of tactics, the outcome was the same – tough, realistic training with heavy oversight and candid feedback.

OPPOSING FORCES

IRAQI

By the beginning of January 1991, the Iraqis had created an impressive-looking defense along the Kuwaiti border. The first tier of this defense was Saddam's line infantry – mostly conscripts who were dug in behind primitive barriers and trenches along the borderlands. The second tier, supporting the line infantry, consisted of Iraqi Army tank and mechanized divisions. Farther behind these divisions, acting as the operational reserve, stood the heavily mechanized units of the Republican Guard.

Of these Iraqi units, the conscript infantry were the least-trained and least-motivated. Many, including Saddam Hussein himself, expected these conscripts to be no more than a speed bump along the coalition forces' advance; and when the ground

war began in February 1991, many of these conscripts happily surrendered to American forces. The Iraqi Army's tank and mechanized forces were competent, but lacked the resources and training that the Republican Guard had received. Ultimately, Saddam Hussein's aim was to have his front-line units impede the coalition forces' advance so as to buy time for the Republican Guard to attack in strength.

Several kilometers away from the advancing US VII Corps was the 18th Mechanized Brigade, part of the 3rd *Tawakalna ala-Allah* Mechanized Division, the latter a key element of the front-line forces of Iraq's Republican Guard. The Republican Guard were the elite shock troops of the Iraqi military – personally loyal to Saddam and privy to the best military equipment in Iraq. Whereas many of the Iraqi Army divisions operated the T-55, T-62, and BRDM-2, the Republican Guard had the BMP-1, BMP-2, and the vaunted T-72. Steven J. Zaloga outlines the paper strength of an Iraqi mechanized battalion in early 1991:

A convoy of destroyed Iraqi BMP-1s in 1991. These vehicles were engaged as they attempted to flee the battle zone. (US Army)

> The standard organization of a BMP mechanized battalion in Iraqi service was 35 BMP-1s (including eight BMP-1K command vehicles), three BTR-63-1 command vehicles (command versions of the Chinese Type 531 APC) and one MT-LB ambulance. During the war, most units were equipped at levels far below the establishment. (Zaloga 1994: 34)

This BMP-1 was photographed in Zahko, Iraq, on April 26, 1991. After the Gulf War, the BMP-1 remained in active service with the Iraqi Army. Here, the two Iraqi soldiers in the foreground prepare to offload the BMP-1 from the back of a heavy transport trailer, most likely in preparation for a training maneuver or for anti-Kurdish operations that were common in northern Iraq throughout the early 1990s. Following the coalition's victory and Saddam's withdrawal from Kuwait, several functioning BMP-1s were captured and shipped to the United States where they served as static displays or Opposing Force (OPFOR) vehicles at the National Training Center. (Photo by Chip HIRES/Gamma-Rapho via Getty Images)

45

BMP-1 GUNNER'S STATION

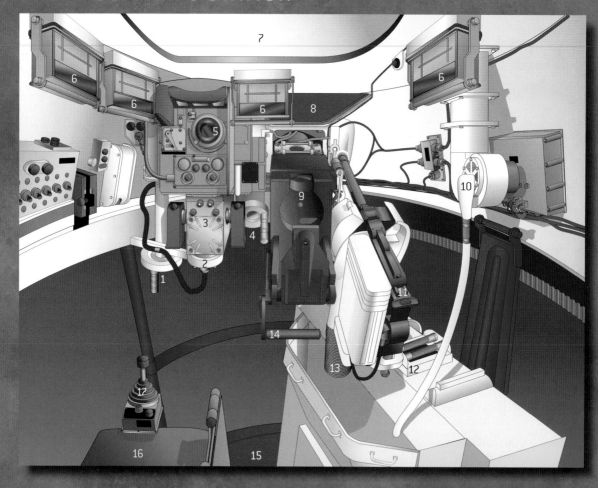

1. Gunner's secondary control (manual traverse)
2. Hydraulic power system
3. Gunner's primary controls
4. Gunner's secondary control (manual elevation)
5. Gunner's primary sight
6. Gunner's periscope
7. Gunner's hatch
8. Malyutka missile launcher access hatch
9. 73mm 2A28 Grom semiautomatic gun breech
10. Extraction fan
11. 7.62mm PKT coaxial machine gun
12. Coaxial machine gun ammunition storage
13. Machine-gun spent cartridge shute and bin
14. Gun breech handle (for cartridge ejection)
15. Floor of turret
16. Gunner's seat
17. Malyutka missile control joystick

M2A2 BRADLEY GUNNER'S STATION

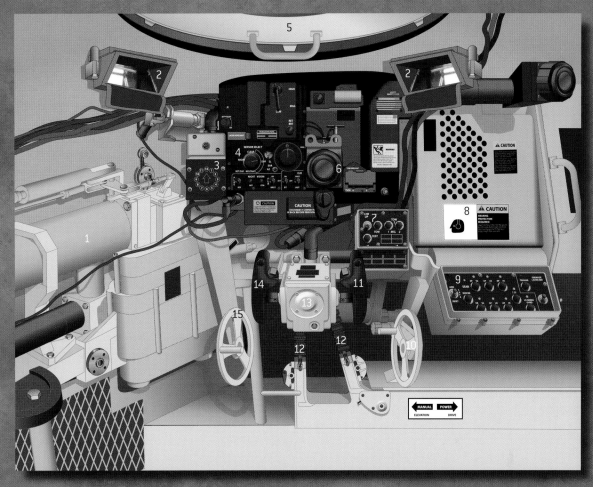

1. Hydraulic fluid reservoir
2. Gunner's periscope
3. Turret orientation indicator
4. Gunner's optical control panel
5. Gunner's hatch
6. Integrated Sight Unit
7. TOW-2 missile control panel
8. Protective panel covering the M242 Bushmaster autocannon and M240C coaxial machine gun

9. Ammunition selector and index panel
10. Gunner's right control handle (manual elevation)
11. Gunner's right control handle (automatic)
12. Dual feeding mechanism for 25mm ammunition
13. Drift modulator
14. Gunner's left control handle (automatic)
15. Gunner's left control handle (manual traverse)

The military police of 3d Brigade, 1st Armored Division (VII Corps) inspect a BMP-1 of the Iraqi Republican Guard damaged during Operation *Desert Storm*. Following the ceasefire, many of the Republican Guard's BMP-1s were found dug into depressed "fighting positions" like this one. (US Army)

The Republican Guard consisted of two corps. The 1st Republican Guard Corps, deployed across southern Iraq and northern Kuwait, consisted of the 1st *Hammurabi* and 2nd *al-Medinah al-Munawera* Armored divisions, the 3rd *Tawakalna ala-Allah* Mechanized Division, and the 4th *Al Faw* Motorized Infantry Division. The 3rd *Tawakalna ala-Allah* Mechanized Division took its name from the Arabic phrase "depending on God" or "God help us." Its mechanized brigades consisted of three mechanized-infantry battalions, each with 45–50 BMPs in the vanguard. The Iraqis set their defenses similar to the Soviet method. Mobile reconnaissance units (equipped with BRDM-2s, MT-LBs, and similar vehicles) stood forward of the Main Line of Resistance. These reconnaissance units were supported by dismounted infantry and artillery observers. Behind these reconnaissance teams, the Iraqis had emplaced minefields, typically 350m (385yd) deep and containing a mix of antitank and anti-personnel mines. However, during the 2d ACR's advance, these mines would prove to be more of a nuisance than a threat. For instance, Lieutenant Mike Hamilton, a tank commander in Eagle Troop, recalled that during the battle of 73 Easting, he heard some muffled explosions coming from underneath his vehicle. Looking over the side of his tank, Hamilton saw what looked like tuna cans scattered across the desert. "These were a bunch of little landmines," he said; and because the tanks and Bradleys were denser than the sand, the mines were blowing *down* instead of blowing up.

Along the Main Line of Resistance, many of the BMPs had been dug into static defensive positions as part of a triangular defensive strongpoint. The bottom two corners either end of the base leg of this triangular defense (separated by 2,000m/2,190yd) faced the enemy. Each corner consisted of at least three BMPs (each assigned to a squad) with interlocking fields of fire. Behind these triangular defenses, the tanks were arrayed in similar fashion, but there was also a tank-heavy reserve in front of the unit's command post. As per doctrine, this reserve took the form of a "coil" – a circular formation with the gun tubes pointed outward.

AMERICAN

Based in Germany, VII Corps had been the premier US Army unit assigned to the defense of Western Europe during the Cold War. By 1990, with the Cold War having ended and the Inner-German Border having disappeared, VII Corps was directed to use its armored assets for the liberation of Kuwait. The units selected for deployment included the 1st Armored Division in Ansbach, the 3d Armored Division in Frankfurt, the 3d Brigade of the 2d Armored Division (forward-stationed in Garlstedt), the 2d ACR in Bamberg, the 11th Aviation Brigade in Illesheim, and the 2d Corps Support Command in Stuttgart. Collectively, this would raise the number of US troops in the Persian Gulf to more than 400,000.

Deploying VII Corps to Operation *Desert Shield* was perhaps the most practical decision the Army could make, for VII Corps was one of the two largest armored contingents within proximity to the theater of operations. As a forward-deployed unit, they were in possession of the Army's most modern equipment, such as the Bradley, M1 Abrams, and the AH-64 Apache attack helicopter. Furthermore, deploying VII Corps gave the Army an opportunity to accelerate the post-Cold War reduction of forces in Western Europe.

The deployment to Saudi Arabia did, however, present a number of problems. A European-based contingent had never undertaken a deployment of this magnitude; thus, by design, VII Corps was never trained for out-of-theater operations. For decades, its mission had been to satisfy the metrics of border duty along the Iron Curtain. Further complicating the issue was the fact that VII Corps' units were scattered across a series of small installations in the German countryside. Whereas the stateside divisions were typically located at one post (e.g. the 82d Airborne Division at Fort Bragg, North Carolina), the European-based divisions were split up into different camps. For instance, the 2d ACR was headquartered in Nuremberg, but its 2d Squadron was located in Bamberg.

Because of the ongoing force reductions and readiness factors, Army planners in some instances had to assemble entire divisions using battalions and brigades borrowed

M3A0 Bradleys from Eagle Troop, 2d Squadron, 2d ACR line up for their initial crew inspections in the Saudi cantonment, December 1990. In the opening months of Operation *Desert Shield*, several thousand US troops (and their armored vehicles) were deployed to Saudi Arabia to deter further aggression from Saddam Hussein. (Chad King)

M3A0 Bradleys from L Troop, 3d Squadron, 3d ACR, line up at the desert motor pool in Saudi Arabia for Operation *Desert Shield*. By January 1991, there were more than 400,000 coalition troops in the desert. Meanwhile, Saddam Hussein showed no signs of bowing to the United Nations' demands for the withdrawal of Iraqi forces from Kuwait. (US Army)

from other units. For example, the 1st Armored Division left behind its 1st Brigade, and borrowed the 3d Infantry Division's 3d Brigade as a replacement. In other instances, units were borrowed from the Army Reserve and National Guard to bring the amalgamated divisions up to full strength.

To effect the deployment of VII Corps assets, the Army gathered some 407 trains with 12,210 railcars to move the thousands of armored vehicles to the ports of embarkation. Staging the tanks and Bradleys at the port of Bremerhaven, the vehicles were loaded onto 154 cargo/troop ships bound for the Persian Gulf. Personnel of the 2d ACR were the first of the VII Corps contingent to arrive in Saudi Arabia, touching down at Dhahran Airfield on December 4, 1990. A few days earlier, the UN Security Council had passed Resolution 678 which gave Saddam Hussein a deadline of January 15 to withdraw his forces from Kuwait, or face military action. Still the Iraqi dictator showed no signs of backing down.

By the beginning of January, however, American ground forces had consolidated their defensive line along the Saudi–Iraqi border. Stretching for more than 240km (150 miles), the front-line coalition forces included XVIII Airborne Corps (the inaugural forces of Operation *Desert Shield*), the amalgamated VII Corps task force, and coalition units including the UK's 1st Armoured Division and France's 6e division légère blindée.

Leading VII Corps' charge into Iraq was the 2d ACR. Independent, heavily armored, and rapidly deployable, the ACR's purpose was to provide armored reconnaissance, surveillance, and mobile security to heavy forces in the field. Unlike conventional armor and infantry units – which are organized (in descending order) into brigades, battalions, and companies – cavalry units are respectively organized into regiments, squadrons, and troops. Each ACR contained three armored cavalry squadrons, an aviation squadron, and a support squadron. An armored cavalry squadron normally consisted of a headquarters troop, three armored cavalry troops, a tank company, and a self-propelled howitzer battery. The ACR's aviation squadron provided aerial reconnaissance and ground-attack capabilities through a combination of AH-64 Apache, UH-60 Black Hawk, and OH-58 Kiowa/Kiowa Warrior helicopters. The support squadron, meanwhile, provided the logistical and

The crew of Eagle 34 (a vehicle belonging to 3d Platoon, Eagle Troop, 2d Squadron, 2d ACR) installs new tracks on their M2A2, Christmas Day 1990. Track and vehicle maintenance were always more difficult in the desert, where the fine grains of sand had a habit of getting caught in every piece of equipment that a soldier owned. (Mike Rhodes)

maintenance assets for the ACR's combat mission. In the months before the Gulf War, the Army had three active ACRs: the 2d, 3d, and 11th. The 2d and 11th ACRs were forward-stationed in Germany, while the 3d ACR resided at Fort Bliss, Texas.

Prior to the Gulf War, the 2d ACR had been equipped with the M3A1, the CFV variant of the Bradley. However, shortly after arriving in Saudi Arabia, the regiment received the new M2A2, shipped into theater in December 1990 and delivered to the forward elements of VII Corps' line. Aside from the M2A2 offering better armor protection and higher top speeds, the scout platoons also received the new TRIMPACK GPS. Although primitive by today's standards, TRIMPACK was then state-of-the-art and significantly increased a unit's situational awareness. The GPS calculations were based on the Military Grid Reference System (divided into denominations of one square kilometer) and gave accurate readings within a few meters of ground truth.

The armored cavalry troop was the centerpiece of the ACR's ground network. Each troop consisted of two tank platoons (each equipped with four M1A1 Abrams tanks) and two mechanized scout platoons (each with six Bradley Fighting Vehicles). Two specially modified M113 APCs comprised the mortar section, whose job was to provide indirect-fire support. The troop's maintenance section had the massive M88 Recovery Vehicle, a tracked behemoth which could tow any disabled vehicle in the Army's inventory. As a testament to their elite subculture within the US Army, the ACRs used their own phonetic alphabet to identify their armored cavalry troops. Thus, instead of Alpha Company, Bravo Company, and Charlie Company, a typical ACR would designate its units as Apache Troop, Bandit Troop, and Crazyhorse Troop.

In a conventional war, the mission of the cavalry troop was to conduct an armored reconnaissance ahead of the main body forces. The Bradleys (and tanks) of the cavalry troop first conduct battlefield surveillance and report the size and disposition of enemy forces to the main body. Then, without becoming decisively engaged, the troop "holds" and "fixes" the enemy force before handing off the fight to the main body. This is accomplished through a "passage of lines," whereby the main body (typically an armored division) flanks or passes through the ACR to complete the destruction of the enemy.

COMBAT

OPENING MOVES: FOX TROOP IN THE LEAD

The commander of VII Corps, Lieutenant General Frederick M. Franks, Jr., himself a cavalryman, understood that in order to engage with the Republican Guard, his corps would have to break through the Iraqis' front-line defenses, rather than being able to bypass them. He and his planners assumed that the enemy could prepare a solid defensive line along much of the Saudi Arabian border. While Major General Thomas G. Rhame's 1st Infantry Division assumed responsibility for breaking into the interior of Iraq, the British 1st Armoured Division would move through Rhame's division and attack the Iraqi reserve to the east; the 2d ACR would perform its intended role as a covering force, leading the 1st and 3d Armored divisions into the breach. A third division – either the 1st Infantry Division or the 1st Cavalry Division – would also join the US attack depending on the outcome of the breaching battle; this was so that Franks' corps could confront the three heavy divisions of the Republican Guard (the 1st *Hammurabi* and 2nd *al-Medinah al-Munawera* Armored divisions plus the 3rd *Tawakalna ala-Allah* Mechanized Division). Even so, the VII Corps ("Jayhawks") plan would change in light of events:

> Franks' divisions were not scheduled to participate in the initial coalition attack on G-day. Their role was to make contact with the Iraqi defenses, get as much of their combat units as possible across the [border] berm, with its actual attack scheduled to start at dawn on 25 February, or G plus 1 … However, because of the coalition's success along the coast, General Schwarzkopf would ask the Jayhawks to change their plans and attack much earlier than anticipated. (Bourque 2001: 205)

Since the front-line Bradley crews weren't equipped to process and handle the influx of enemy prisoners, the Bradleys of 2d Squadron, 2d ACR simply ferried the POWs back to the rear echelon where they could be processed by the nearest military-police unit. Here, Eagle 36 (an M2A2 belonging to 3d Scout Platoon, Eagle Troop, 2d Squadron, 2d ACR) delivers a horde of Iraqi POWs to the rear area of the 2d ACR's advance. (Danny Davis)

On Saturday, February 23, the 2d ACR occupied the western sector of VII Corps' front line, south of the border berm. The regiment's mission that day was to "conduct a zone reconnaissance forward of the berm and clear lanes in it for the two following American armored divisions. The regiment's radio nets came alive at 1310, when, for the first time since May 1945, the oldest mounted unit on continuous active service in the U.S. Army began moving in battle formation" (Bourque 2001: 199–200). During the early afternoon 2d Squadron, 2d ACR moved into Iraq with Fox Troop in the vanguard, and soon made contact with elements of the 1st Infantry Division. The regiment encountered minimal opposition, but two of its personnel were wounded by an unexploded munition. On their first day in Iraq the 2d ACR hadn't met a single enemy vehicle or troop. Private First Class Matthew Lee, the driver aboard Eagle 33 (the third Bradley of 3d Scout Platoon, Eagle Troop) recalled that "as soon as we crossed that berm, I thought we were going right into the teeth of the Iraqi Army, with gunshots and artillery, but there was *nothing* there … it was anti-climactic. I thought for sure that it was going to be Hell on Earth as soon as we crossed the berm." But for the men of the 2d Squadron, 2d ACR, there was nothing out there but empty desert.

On Sunday, February 24, the second day of the 2d ACR's advance, Eagle, Fox, and Ghost troops encountered only sporadic Iraqi resistance, most of it dismounted. As Captain H.R. McMaster, commanding Eagle Troop, recalled:

> Enroute to our new objective, Captain Tom Sprowls' Fox Troop called "contact" over the radio. Their lead scout platoon, led by Lieutenant T.J. Linzy had received fire and killed two of the enemy. The rest surrendered. The squadron continued its move. The intelligence officer, Captain Rhett Scott, estimated that Fox Troop had encountered the scouts or security forces of an Iraqi infantry division protecting their army's western flank. (McMaster n.d.: 4–5)

Much to the Americans' surprise, however, most of the enemy troops were surrendering in droves. Iraqi front-line soldiers would do little more than fire a few shots then throw down their weapons, shouting "President Bush! President Bush!" These supposedly "battle-hardened" Iraqis were more "battle-weary" by the time US ground forces arrived.

At 0640hrs on Monday, February 25, the 2d ACR resumed its advance; the Americans engaged dug-in enemy infantry and captured more prisoners, taking Objective GATES by 1230hrs. That afternoon, Ghost Troop encountered Iraqi vehicles. As First Lieutenant John Hillen (Assistant S3, 2d Squadron, 2d ACR) stated: "At 1400 hours, Ghost Troop engaged and destroyed a MTLB-equipped Republican Guards reconnaissance company. 1LT Mecca, Ghost Troop XO, later brought six captured MTLBs to the squadron's forward command post" (Hillen 1991: 10).

By the evening of February 25, the 2d ACR had halted its advance along the 50 Easting. In the featureless deserts of southern Iraq, the only way VII Corps could track its movement was by using the longitudinal gridlines on a map known as "eastings." Meanwhile, the 2d ACR had adjusted the configuration of its front-line forces, giving the 2d Squadron a 10km (6-mile) front, which Major Douglas Macgregor, the squadron operations officer, said gave his troops half the frontage they had previously had during the first few days of the operation. Maneuvering across that small of a front would facilitate the use of the dreaded "box" formation. Macgregor recalled that none of the troops liked the "box," as it meant their forces would crash headlong into the enemy like a Napoleonic column.

From the Iraqi perspective, the Republican Guard's 3rd *Tawakalna ala-Allah* Mechanized Division was in place in a blocking position about 130km (80 miles) from Kuwait City. It had suffered greatly from the coalition air campaign, but was ready for a fight on the 26th. Attacked from several directions, the men of the 3rd *Tawakalna ala-Allah* Mechanized Division would have "little opportunity to do anything but either surrender or fight and die in place. They chose the latter course" (Bourque 1997). The Iraqi defense was organized into three zones: the operations zone contained the bulk of the defensive position; the security zone lay between the operations zone and the advancing coalition forces; and the rear zone was where the main logistics effort was made. After sending out reconnaissance forces, the commander of the 3rd *Tawakalna ala-Allah* Mechanized Division ordered a reinforced battalion into the security zone during the early hours of February 26: "Organized into company and platoon strongpoints, these units were to break up the US attack, cause it to slow down, and inform the division commander on the nature of the enemy advance" (Bourque 1997). In the operations zone, the Iraqi commander employed his three main brigades:

> On the left flank he positioned the 18th Mechanized Brigade. South of the 18th Mechanized Brigade, and in front of a major supply depot located on the IPSA Pipeline Road twenty kilometers north of the Saudi Arabian border, were the remnants of the Iraqi 37th Armored Brigade from the 12th Armored Division. The 9th Armored Brigade, reinforced by survivors from the 50th Armored Brigade, held the center of the Tawakalna line … The 29th Brigade defended the right flank of the division's sector. The 29th Brigade had no other units protecting its right flank. Without such protection, American forces were free to attack it from the north without fear of encountering Iraqi units prepared to conduct an effective defense. (Bourque 1997)

It was on the Iraqis' left flank – the 18th Mechanized Brigade sector – that the 2d ACR's battle was to take place. By sunrise on the morning of Tuesday, February 26, the 2d ACR and the front-line forces of the 3rd *Tawakalna ala-Allah* Mechanized Division lay only 14km (9 miles) apart. By this time, Eagle and Ghost troops had replaced Fox Troop in the lead. At 0800hrs, Ghost Troop engaged and destroyed the surviving elements of the reconnaissance force it had encountered on the previous day. During the late morning, the 2d Squadron was ordered to move first to "the 52, then the 55, then the 57 Easting. At approximately 1200hrs, the 2d ACR received orders to press on with the attack toward the 70 Easting. The 2d ACR would turn 90 degrees and attack eastward to fix the main body of the *Tawakalna ala-Allah* Division. The regiment was to avoid any decisive engagement with the Iraqis, however: the mission was to "hold and fix" against the Republican Guard before handing off the battle to the 1st Infantry Division, whose armor battalions would deliver the crushing blow. Meanwhile, the 3d Armored Division would swing north to envelop the enemy along his flanks.

An M3 Bradley – one of the few not swapped for the M2A2 – commanded by First Lieutenant John Mecca, the executive officer of Ghost Troop, 2d Squadron, 2d ACR, maneuvers past two abandoned MT-LB multi-purpose tracked vehicles during a lull in the fight at 73 Easting. Aside from the BMP-1s, the Republican Guard placed many of the lighter-armored MT-LBs at the vanguard of their defense. (Douglas Macgregor)

GHOST TROOP'S SECTOR

The first direct-fire contact of the battle of 73 Easting came at around 1500hrs on Tuesday, February 26. As it had been during the previous days' advance, most of the Iraqi fire was from dismounted small arms; but as Eagle and Ghost troops of the 2d ACR approached the 71 Easting, the enemy's armored vehicles finally came into play. Three T-72 tanks were quickly destroyed, and shortly after 1530hrs the 2d Squadron, 2d ACR encountered a battalion strongpoint:

Strong points consisted of dug in vehicle and soldier fighting positions, wire, mines and prepared field of fire. In most cases the Iraqi units were in the right place, but had not developed their positions as well as they should have … It was a short, but violent battle … US scout platoons followed the M1 tanks providing "scratching fires" to protect the US tanks from the Iraqi infantry. Just as the 2nd Squadron arrived at the rear of the battalion strong point the Iraqis launched a counterattack. While brave, it was ineffective. In 23 minutes one troop from the US squadron destroyed over half of the Iraqi battalion. (Bourque 1997)

At about the same time the 3d Squadron, 2d ACR attacked the southern part of the same strongpoint; at about 1645hrs, a company of T-72 tanks counterattacked the 3d Squadron, but they opened fire at too great a range and the rounds hit the ground ahead of the American vehicles. At a range of 2,100m (2,300yd) the Abrams tanks engaged and destroyed most the Iraqi armor. The Iraqis fought hard, but were clearly surprised by the speed of the American advance; this meant they were unable to prepare their defenses adequately. The 2d ACR now moved to the defense:

Franks' orders to Colonel Don Holder, the 2nd Armored Cavalry Regiment commander, were to avoid a decisive engagement. Holder's troops had successfully destroyed one Iraqi battalion strong point, but there were still at least six or seven more battalions waiting for the US regiment, which did not have the combat power to break through the Tawakalna's defenses. Holder, therefore ordered his squadrons to hold at their current positions and prepare to pass the 1st Infantry Division, which had moved behind the Regiment, forward. (Bourque 1997)

By 1700hrs on the evening of February 26, Ghost Troop's tanks and Bradleys had consolidated along the 73 Easting. By all accounts, their opening forays into the battle had been superb. The M1A1 Abrams tanks of Lieutenant Andy Kilgore's 2d Tank Platoon had cut down nearly a dozen BMP-1s and dispatched several T-72s.

On the far left flank of Ghost Troop's advance was the 1st Scout Platoon under the command of Lieutenant Keith Garwick. Shortly after consolidating his six Bradleys on-line, Garwick called on his platoon to assume their predetermined sectors of fire. Establishing these sectors of fire was a critical task for any Bradley in a defensive position. Every space on the battlefield had to be covered by a vehicle's crew-served weapon – be it the main gun, the TOW missile launcher, or the coaxial machine gun. Every Bradley therefore had a specified area of the battlespace for which it was responsible for engaging targets. The two Bradleys on the far left of the formation, Garwick's Ghost 11 and Ghost 15, scanned their guns from the center of the battlefield to the extreme left of the squadron's sector. For the two Bradleys occupying the center, Ghost 16 scanned from the left to the center while Ghost 14 scanned from center-right. The remaining two Bradleys, Ghost 12 and Ghost 13, scanned from the center toward the right.

Barely a few moments after picking up their sectors of fire, Garwick reported to Captain Joseph Sartiano, Ghost Troop's commander, that a dozen tanks and BMPs had appeared over the horizon at a range of about 3,500m (3,830yd) – and they were closing in on Ghost Troop's position. At around 1800hrs, as the sun set and the poor

OPPOSITE   VII Corps' sector, evening of February 26, 1991.

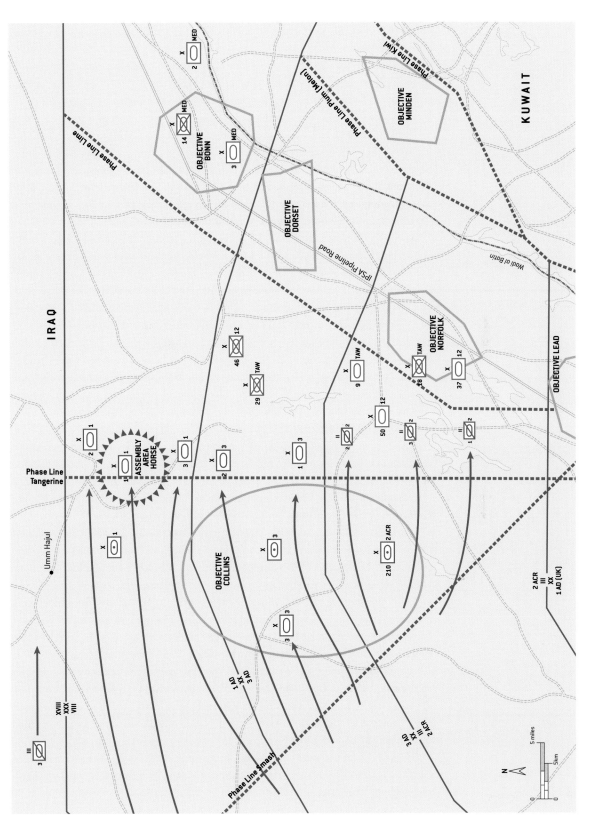

visibility conditions persisted, the Iraqis mounted a determined attack employing dismounted infantry, T-55 and T-72 tanks, and armored transports. Since these Iraqi vehicles were in the US 3d Armored Division's zone of attack, Sartiano told Garwick to establish "positive identification" before engaging the BMPs. Elsewhere along the coalition's battlefront, there had been some tragic incidents of fratricide involving the Bradley. Friendly tank commanders and aircraft pilots – many of whom were fighting off delirium because of a lack of sleep – had mistakenly engaged a handful of Bradleys, believing them to be either BMPs or ZSU 23-4 self-propelled anti-aircraft guns. Sartiano was determined not to have any such incidents occur in Ghost Troop's sector. Moments later, Ghost Troop's executive officer, First Lieutenant John Mecca, came over the radio with confirmation that the advance elements of the 3d Armored Division were still an hour away. The sector was clear to engage.

At ranges of more than 3,000m (3,280yd), Garwick knew that he could not effectively engage the BMPs with his 25mm main gun; he would have to rely on the TOW missiles. As it was throughout much of Saddam Hussein's mechanized forces, these offending IFVs were the base-model BMP-1s; still, the BMP-1's 73mm main gun could disable a Bradley at ranges of up to 1,000m (1,095yd). Garwick also kept in mind that he had to save most of his TOW missiles for the priority targets: the T-72s. In theory, the Bradley could not stand toe-to-toe with a T-72, or any other main battle tank. In a contest of fire, a Bradley's only hope for survival was to engage the heavier armored vehicles with a TOW missile from standoff ranges of more than 2km (1.2 miles).

As Garwick picked up the first BMP-1 in his sights, he began the drill of issuing fire commands. Within the confines of the turret, the commander and gunner were expected to work interdependently to acquire and engage targets. Each man could acquire and engage a target from his respective station and Garwick, as the commander, had the capability to control the turret and the main gun independent of the gunner. Garwick began the first of his fire commands the same way he had done at countless gunneries on the firing ranges in Germany: "Gunner, Missile, PC!"

"Gunner!" – the crew alert was the first part of his normal fire command – alerted the crewman who was expected to engage the target. "Missile!" indicated that the gunner was to select the TOW missile. On other occasions, the commander would say "Sabot!" indicating that the gunner was to select the armor-piercing 25mm rounds, or "HE!" (pronounced "H-E") indicating the use of a high-explosive round. At closer ranges, armor-piercing sabot rounds were the ammunition of choice, as they were the most effective at stopping light-armored vehicles. The high-explosive rounds, while effective on smaller targets and enemy positions, had virtually no effect on a BMP. "PC!" (indicating a personnel carrier) was the final part of the fire command, simply identifying the target for the gunner, who by this point, had probably already identified the enemy vehicle. Thus, a medley of "Gunner, Missile, PC!" and "Gunner Missile, Tank!" came over the intercoms of Ghost Troop's front-line Bradleys as they engaged their targets of opportunity.

Meanwhile, on Garwick's right flank, Sergeant Ricardo Garcia, the commander of Ghost 12, calmly deployed the first of eight TOW missiles into a medley of Iraqi tanks and BMP-1s at a range 3,600m (3,940yd) to his direct front. Launching the TOW missile, Garcia issued his fire commands with the steadiness of second nature. With a

quick "Gunner, Missile, Tank!" Garcia guided the gunner of Ghost 12 onto the targets. Under the glow of the Bradley's thermal sight, the gunner espied the unmistakable heat signature of an Iraqi T-72. Barely three seconds later, the T-72 exploded in a brilliant flash of blue and orange flames. With one T-72 down, Garcia repeated the drill against a BMP-1 with the same result.

From the looks of the battlefield, Garcia and the other Bradley crewmen could tell that the Iraqis were startled and confused by the onset of American armor. Half of the Republican Guard force seemed to be counterattacking (albeit unsuccessfully and with no tactical bearing) while the other half seemed to be fleeing the battlefield. Whatever their disposition, the Iraqis were presenting nothing but easy targets for the Ghost Troop Bradley crews. Indeed, several BMPs were travelling *perpendicular* to Ghost Troop's position – offering slow-moving silhouettes that resembled the gunnery targets from the firing ranges in Germany. Engaging targets under these conditions, some Bradley commanders remarked that this part of the war felt like just another training exercise.

But as Garwick's platoon fired their missiles down range, he remembered that he could also use indirect fire to kill the enemy vehicles (or at least disrupt their movement) before they got any closer to Ghost Troop's lead echelon. Over the radio net, he appealed for artillery support. Thanks to the squadron's Combat Observation Lasing Team (COLT), mounted atop their M981 fire support vehicle, Garwick confirmed the distance of the Iraqi formation at 3,600m (3,940yd). With distance and direction verified, First Lieutenant Mecca and Ghost Troop's Fire Support Officer, Lieutenant Joe Deskevich, radioed the squadron's Fire Support Cell to get the M109

Here, M109 Paladin self-propelled howitzers and M992 field artillery ammunition supply vehicles of the 1st Armored Division are pictured on February 5, 1991. According to Major Douglas Macgregor, 2d Squadron's operations officer, at 73 Easting the Fire Direction Officer of the 6th Battalion, 41st Field Artillery had "tactical control" of the self-propelled howitzers of the 2d Squadron, 2d ACR, even though most of the M109s involved belonged to the squadron's battery. (Photo by Win Mcnamee/Department of Defense (DOD)/The LIFE Picture Collection/ Getty Images)

Paladin self-propelled howitzers' 155mm rounds on target. At first, however, Fire Support said "No" – the impact area was in the 3d Armored Division's intended zone of attack. Luckily, the Fire Direction Officer for 6th Battalion, 41st Field Artillery was aware that the 3d Armored Division was still hours behind the 2d ACR's advance, and overruled the Fire Support Cell. Thus, with the blessing of the Fire Direction Officer, the 155mm rounds were on their way in a matter of seconds.

Perched atop the commander's seat of his Bradley, Garwick watched as the rounds disrupted and killed several more enemy BMPs creeping toward his sector. For the soldiers of Garwick's 1st Scout Platoon, it was the first time any of them had ever seen the 155mm Dual-Purpose Improved Conventional Munition (DPICM) round in action. The DPICM was essentially a cluster bomb which could, depending on its caliber, be used for anti-personnel or anti-armor purposes. The 155mm howitzer-delivered variants were especially devastating and Garwick's scouts were awestruck at the effect the rounds were having on the Iraqi vehicles. Major Macgregor likened it to "a thousand exploding baseballs" crashing into a target.

Hearing Garwick's contact reports over the radio, Captain Sartiano moved his tank northward to join Garwick on-line, scrambling the rest of Ghost Troop to provide direct-fire support to the 1st Scout Platoon. This scrambling maneuver integrated the 2d Platoon tanks into Garwick's formation, turning the American line into a so-called "viper team" – a combined-arms firing team of four tanks and six Bradleys. As Kilgore's tanks settled into the viper team, his tank gunners shot their laser rangefinders into the offending mix of 11 BMPs and nine tanks. Unanimously confirming the range at 3,000m (3,280yd), Kilgore's four tanks began firing sabot rounds into the Iraqi vehicles. But Garwick in Ghost 11, and his wingman, Sergeant Kevin Robbins in Ghost 15, had their own agenda. Picking up another BMP-1 in his sights, Garwick issued the fire command for yet another TOW missile engagement. Hearing the mechanical choreography of the TOW launcher rise from its retracted position was a familiar sound for any Bradley commander. However, in the heat of combat, the process of deploying the TOW missile seemed excruciatingly slow. This was compounded by the fact that the Bradley had to remain stationary while the TOW missile was in flight and the gunner had to optically guide the missile to its target with a steady hand. In the years following Operation *Desert Storm*, the Bradley crewmen were unanimous in their complaints that the Bradley did not have a "fire-and-forget" missile system – but on February 26, 1991, the gunners of Ghost 11 and Ghost 15 deployed their TOW missiles with deadly precision.

Hearing the hiss of the TOW missile as it left its respective launcher, Garwick and Robbins could feel their Bradley shudder in the wake of each missile's deployment. The two gunners, eyeing the trajectory through the red glow of the thermal viewfinder, maintained their white-knuckle grip on the fire controls as they made steady corrections to the warheads' trajectories. Seconds later, the broadside two BMP-1s erupted in flames as the vehicles sputtered to a halt.

By this time, Garwick's training had taken over; he was delivering the fire commands with the speed and accuracy that could only be gained through rigorous repetition. Yet seeing that this was his first engagement against live targets that could shoot back, Garwick was understandably shaken. Those listening to Garwick on the radio could sense it, too. From the driver's seat of Ghost 14, 18-year-old Private First

Class Jason E. Kick recorded his observations in real time. Speaking into a tape recorder he had taken along for the journey, Kick reported that: "This is chaos here. This is total chaos. Red 1 [Garwick], he's the platoon leader. You can hear it in his voice, he's all shook up." But shaken as he was, Garwick suppressed his emotions and plowed through his fire commands, all while processing the contact reports from the other five vehicles in his platoon.

A member of Ghost Troop, 2d Squadron, 2d ACR inspects a partially destroyed BMP-1 within its defensive position following the battle of 73 Easting. (Joe Deskevich)

Fifteen minutes after Garwick's initial contact report, Ghost Troop's "viper team" Bradleys reported that all Iraqi targets had been destroyed. In the contest of fire, the Bradley had not only proven itself against the BMP-1, but against the vaunted T-72 as well. But as Garwick's and Kilgore's platoons cheered the destruction of the enemy's vehicles, some of the displaced Iraqis were catching their second wind.

Suddenly, after several moments of silence along the battlefront, two 73mm BMP-1 shells struck the desert floor in front of Ghost 16 and Ghost 14 – the two Bradleys on Garwick's right flank. Where were these Iraqi rounds coming from? Garwick and Kilgore had confirmed that all enemy vehicles in front of them had been destroyed, either by direct fire or from the artillery barrage. Had they somehow missed a vehicle? Had enemy reinforcements arrived? Whatever the case may have been, Garwick alerted his platoon for action.

From the turret of Ghost 16, Staff Sergeant Don Chaffee (commander) and Sergeant Andrew Moller (gunner) readied their vehicle for a second round of trading fire with the enemy. The Bradleys on either side of Ghost 16 noticed that their wingman was in a dangerous position, however, the vehicle sitting atop a spur that ran parallel to the 73 Easting. In the featureless deserts of Iraq, a rise of even a few meters is militarily significant. It can mean the difference between life and death for a defending force; and considering that one (or more) enemy vehicles were now lurking in the low ground, Ghost 16 was at risk of drawing enemy fire. According to the battle logs, however, Chaffee moved Ghost 16 farther forward, most likely to get a clearer shot at the offending enemy who had just fired into Ghost Troop's sectors. This maneuver made Ghost 16 even more vulnerable to enemy fire.

Aghast at what was happening, Kilgore scrambled for the radio aboard his tank and screamed, "16, you're skylined! Back down, over!" Ghost 16 was indeed skylined: the term refers to a vehicle sitting atop a piece of high ground, offering a prominent

silhouette to whoever looked upon it from the ground below. Positioned on the ridge, Ghost 16 was perfectly silhouetted against the residual early-evening light, increased by the numerous knocked-out vehicles burning on the battlefield. Combined with the Bradley's dangerously high profile, Ghost 16's position meant that the Bradley presented an easy target for whichever enemy vehicle was lurking below the ridgeline.

What the crew of Ghost 16 didn't know, however, was that the offending BMP-1 was situated directly in front of them, 500–600m (545–655yd) away on the low ground ahead of the ridge. The vehicle had been hit by a sabot round from Kilgore's tank platoon earlier in the fight. However, since the 120mm sabot round was a "kinetic energy" projectile, it would often slice through a target without causing it to explode. Such was the case with this lone BMP-1: the sabot round from Kilgore's platoon had ripped through the vehicle, killing one or more of the crew, but the vehicle itself remained intact and the 73mm main gun was still operational. Thus, either a surviving member of the original BMP-1 crew or a wayward dismount from another vehicle had climbed into the turret and was taking aim at Ghost Troop's front line. The first two rounds had hit the desert floor – hardly surprising considering the Iraqis' poor gunnery skills – but now that Ghost 16 was standing perfectly still, and silhouetted against the evening sky, the next shots fired from this BMP would not be "grounders."

Suddenly, the crew of Ghost 16 felt their Bradley rocked by a sudden jolt. Whatever had just hit their vehicle, the force of the impact was such that it knocked the vehicle more than 3ft backward. Although no one aboard Ghost 16 knew it, the lone BMP-1 to their direct front had just fired its main-gun round – and it impacted just to the right of the driver's compartment. Despite the sudden daze, however, Ghost 16's crew had not suffered any casualties. In the turret, Sergeant Moller looked toward his commander, Staff Sergeant Chaffee, and shouted "What the f*** was that?!?!" Yet before Chaffee could even answer, or scan the horizon for the perpetrator, the BMP-1 fired its next round at Ghost 16. A fraction of a second later, the 73mm round tore through the Bradley's turret, killing Sergeant Andrew Moller.

In the driver's seat of Ghost 16, Private First Class Patrick Bledsoe was just as shocked as his vehicle commander. He had felt the impact of the first 73mm blast as it rocked the Bradley, and could feel the residual heat of the second blast as it landed just inches above the driver's compartment. At first, Bledsoe had no indication that any of his colleagues had been killed, but given the severity of the impact, he wasn't optimistic. He yelled through the intercom to see if anyone was still alive. When he received no answer, he jumped from the driver's seat and ran to Ghost 14 where he pounded on the rear hatch of the Bradley until it opened. Visibly shaken, Bledsoe grimly told the dismounts of Ghost 14, "We just got hit! I think Sergeant Moller's dead."

Watching this situation unfold from the commander's station of the COLT vehicle, Sergeant Larry Foltz, a towering man with a bodybuilder physique, dismounted his vehicle and made a beeline dash to the disabled Bradley, not knowing whether he'd find any survivors. Lieutenant Kilgore, from atop his tank, provided covering fire while Foltz made his way toward the stricken vehicle. But Foltz was worried about much more than just enemy fire – judging from the appearance of Ghost 16, he knew he was in a race against time before the vehicle exploded. The Bradley had already caught fire and it was only a matter of minutes before the flames would ignite the TOW missiles. Initially, Foltz attempted to open the rear door of the Bradley. When

Two BMP-1s destroyed by Ghost Troop, 2d Squadron, 2d ACR, February 27, 1991. One of the BMP-1s is situated on the reverse slope of a sand dune. Although most of the terrain surrounding 73 Easting was flat, featureless desert, Ghost Troop's area had several dunes and ridges which made it easier for some enemy vehicles to hide. (Joe Deskevich)

that proved unsuccessful, he jumped on the back deck of the vehicle and began pounding away at the rear cargo hatch. There, however, he encountered a different problem: the force of the impact from the 73mm round had literally jammed the cargo hatch shut. Undeterred by the situation, however, Foltz simply grabbed a nearby "tanker's bar" – a 6ft-long steel rod that tank crewmen use to lift the M1 Abrams' track blocks – and furiously beat and pried the hatch until it opened. Reaching inside, Foltz pulled out the survivors of Ghost 16 – Staff Sergeant Chaffee plus Specialist Terry Lorson and Specialist Tim Tomlinson, the dismounted observers – who were later taken aboard Ghost 15. For his actions, Foltz would be awarded the Silver Star Medal.

First Lieutenant Mecca recalled hearing the announcement of Sergeant Moller's tragic demise: "All of a sudden, the whole troop net went silent." Thus far, it had been a one-sided battle and none of the Ghost Troop soldiers could fathom how suddenly one of their own had met his death. Despite the shock, however, Lieutenant Garwick was able to take control of the situation. Suppressing his own anxiety, he keyed the radio and announced: "Keep fighting. Don't lose focus! Keep fighting, out!" Ghost Troop was able to rally around Sergeant Moller's death and continued pressing forward beyond the 73 Easting. However, the tragedy of his passing and Ghost 16's demise was made worse by yet another incident of "friendly fire." Hours after Chaffee, Lorson, and Tomlinson had been evacuated from the vehicle, Hawk Company (2d Squadron's tank company) arrived along the 73 Easting to relieve Ghost Troop. The lead tank in Hawk Company's formation mistook the disabled Ghost 16 for an enemy vehicle, and laid a 120mm round into the smoldering Bradley, where Sergeant Moller's body still lay.

EAGLE TROOP'S SECTOR

Meanwhile, in Eagle Troop's sector of the battle, the Bradleys of 1st and 3d Scout platoons were cutting a wide swath of destruction:

> In the southern portion of the zone, at approximately the 68 Easting, Eagle encountered prepared defenses in zone, with dug-in infantry in bunkers and tanks in revetted positions … Eagle led with its tanks and punched through the enemy defenses quickly, and destroyed more than 20 tanks and other armored vehicles, as well as several bunkers

and supporting infantry … During this attack, a sandstorm and mist cut visibility to 800–1000m [875–1,095yd], but thermal sights could easily identify enemy out to 3000 meters [3,280yd]. This provided the squadron with an incredible advantage throughout the fighting. (Hillen 1991: 10–11)

Traveling on the northern edge of Eagle Troop's sector, Eagle 13 and Eagle 16 spotted a pair of Iraqi tanks. Staff Sergeant Cowart Magee, the commander of Eagle 16, contacted First Lieutenant Danny Davis, the Fire Support Officer whose FIST-V armored artillery observation vehicle was close behind Eagle 16. As Davis later stated, "He called me on the radio and told me he had something in his thermal sights he could not quite identify … I pulled up alongside him and jumped into his turret. As I focused the red screen, I opened my eyes wide in disbelief." The two enemy AFVs were T-72 main battle tanks. "Because of the horrible visibility created by the dust storm, the enemy – without the benefit of thermal viewfinders – still was unaware of our position." Davis returned to his Fire Support Team Vehicle thinking, "My first kill of the day!" Moments later, a fireball nearby made Davis think that Eagle 16 had sustained a hit. In fact, Sergeant Roland Moody, Eagle 16's gunner, had just fired a TOW missile at one of the T-72s. "No!" Davis cried, "Those are my tanks! I get to kill them!" But it was too late. The TOW missile's impact on the Iraqi tank detonated the T-72's ammunition rack and blew its turret skywards. Meanwhile, the gunner aboard Staff Sergeant James Lawrence's Eagle 13, Sergeant Brad Feltman, prepared to engage the other enemy tank with a TOW missile. Eagle 13's driver, Private First Class Dave Pronti, witnessed the second T-72's destruction: "The turret of this T-72 came off and was flipping like a bottle cap in the air and when it landed, the whole thing burst into flames."

Having dealt decisively with the pair of T-72s, Eagle 13 and Eagle 16 continued their advance. Lawrence's Bradley soon encountered an emplaced BMP-1. According to Pronti, "The BMP was so low into the ground that it couldn't elevate its gun to engage us and we couldn't depress low enough to engage it … So we had to back up to engage it." Throwing the gear selector into reverse, Pronti slammed his foot on the gas pedal until the M2A2 Bradley was about 50m (55yd) from the BMP. Every man aboard Eagle 13 was surprised they hadn't seen the BMP-1 earlier, and why the vehicle was dug so low into its defensive position as to be rendered ineffective. Swinging the turret hard right, Feltman yelled "Identify!" as he depressed the 25mm autocannon as far as it would go. Picking up the BMP-1 in his sights, he saw the enemy vehicle trying desperately to traverse its own turret and elevate its own gun, yet hindered from doing so because of its position in the poorly planned fighting hole. With armor-piercing sabot rounds at the ready, Feltman yelled "On the way!" as he depressed the trigger, firing a multi-round burst into the struggling BMP-1. Although Feltman and his fellow scouts had been confident in their equipment, none of them quite knew how the Soviet-made BMP-1 would stand up against direct fire from a Bradley, so seeing the flurry of 25mm sabot rounds pepper and destroy the hapless BMP-1 came as quite a shock.

The dug-in BMP-1 was quickly dispatched by Eagle 13's main gun, but "as we passed by one of the entrenched positions, a few soldiers jumped out and tried to take pot-shots with an RPG." Private First Class Emil Bagalso, one of the dismounted

scouts riding in the rear of Eagle 13, was alert to such a possibility. When a solitary Iraqi soldier, armed with an RPG, appeared from cover and sought to engage Eagle 13 from the rear, Bagalso would have none of it. Using one of the M2A2's firing ports, the young scout quickly dispatched the lone attacker with a burst from his M16A2 rifle.

Meanwhile, the other Bradleys in the 1st and 3d platoons went to work firing TOW missiles and 25mm rounds into the various BMP-1s that emerged from the fog of battle. Having engaged multiple targets during the day, Eagle 36 was running low on high-explosive ammunition. Traveling in Eagle 36, young Private Michael Tribble, the junior-ranking dismount aboard the vehicles, had tirelessly loaded ammunition belts throughout the battle:

> The sounds and smells of the battlefield didn't affect him: he continued to be intensely focused on feeding the Bradley's ammunition. However, when Eagle 36 fired its second TOW missile, Tribble's courage would be put to the test. The Bradley's twin-mounted TOW missile was a potent weapon, but it had to be reloaded manually after every engagement … To reload the TOW, the scout would have to dismount the Bradley with extra TOW missiles in hand, and stand atop the vehicle while inserting them into the launch tubes. It was a nerve-racking process, especially if the Bradley was engaged in a firefight. During situations like this, the life expectancy of a dismounted scout was approximately thirty seconds. But without hesitation, Tribble threw open the back hatch of the Bradley and jumped onto the TOW launcher, shoving the two missiles into their respective tubes. Bullets were whizzing past his head and he could hear several more pinging off the Bradley's front end; the enemy fire was closing in on him. "At this point, my adrenaline was going a mile a minute," he said, "slamming home the TOW missile and closing the hatch." Once back inside the vehicle, Tribble screamed into the intercom, "Up!" – alerting the gunner that the TOW launcher was reloaded and ready for action. (Guardia 2015: 166)

BMP-1 SIGHTS

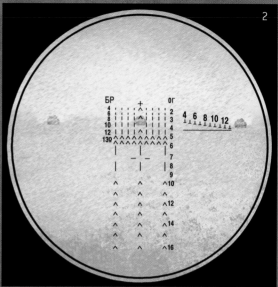

The target acquisition and firing process of the BMP-1 did not benefit from the same technology aboard the M2A2 Bradley. For instance, the BMP-1 did not have a thermal imaging system, nor even a decent fire-control system. The main gun was notoriously inaccurate at stand-off distances, and the Iraqis' poor maintenance program only made the situation worse.

For target acquisition, the BMP-1 gunner (the lone man in the turret) had to scan the battle space for enemy targets. Because the BMP-1 had no active range finder, the gunner had to rely on the reticle's graduated hash marks to determine the distance. While the reticle was barely adequate in optimal visibility conditions (**1**), it did not cope well with poor visibility (**2**). The BMP-1 did have a 1PN22M1 night sight, but it could only see up to 400m (435yd) and could not be adequately used during low-visibility daylight operations.

When the target was identified, the gunner selected the ammunition for the engagement, either the OG-15V or the PG-15V depending on the type of target. Normally, the BMP-1 gunner would rely on the automatic loader but the system was complex, prone to breakdown, and often snagged any loose-fitting parts of a crewman's uniform. Thus, the Iraqis (like many who received the BMP-1 exports) simply removed the autoloader as they found they could the projectiles faster by hand.

BRADLEY SIGHTS

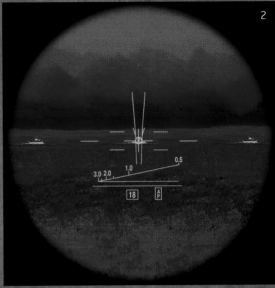

The M2A2 Bradley could see farther than any Soviet-built IFV on the Iraqi battlefront. Inside the turret of the Bradley, the gunner was equipped with a Raytheon Integrated Sight Unit (ISU) which had options for day and thermal sights. In either mode, the gunner could identify targets at magnifications of 4× ("low mag") and 12× ("high mag"). An optical extension relay copied the image of the gunner's sight to the commander. The gunner also had periscopes for forward and side observation.

The process of acquiring a target was aided by the Bradley's superior optics for both daytime (**1**) and low-visibility (**2**) engagements. When the gunner identified a target to engage with the 25mm Bushmaster gun, he had to align it within the dot and crosshairs of the aiming reticle. Almost simultaneously, the gunner would determine the range and type of ammunition for the engagement. The gunner could choose "HE" or "AP" for the 25mm engagement. The type of ammunition could be verified on the gunsight itself. Note the red rectangle on the lower right side of the reticle, outlining the words "AP." With the reticle properly aligned over the target, the gunner depressed the

trigger after announcing "On the Way!" — alerting the crew that the enemy target was about to be engaged. Because many of the AP and HE ammunition belts were equipped with tracer rounds, the gunner had the ability to correct the lay of the 25mm gun and guide the remaining rounds toward the target.

At night, or during periods of low visibility, the Bradley's thermal imaging system gave an infrared signature of any target within normal range of the armament. The target acquisition and firing sequence were the same as during the day-sight operations but the gunner had to be more judicious in his target selection — heat silhouettes did not lend themselves to easy identification and could lead to "false positives" and incidents of fratricide.

During periods of "degraded gunnery," when the optics and/or range finders were not working, the bottom reticle (the acute angle with hashed numbers across the top) was used to "choke" the target. When the entire silhouette fit between the two lines of the acute angle (bottom and top of the vehicle touching the respective lines), the range was approximated by looking at the closest hashed number.

The view from Private First Class Matthew Lee's driver seat as he steers Eagle 33, an M2A2, forward through the battlefield where an Iraqi T-72 burns after being hit by a Bradley's TOW missile. The destructive power of the TOW missile was a shock to those who had never seen it used in combat. Not only did it make short order of the BMPs, it virtually obliterated the enemy main battle tanks. (Matthew Lee)

With the TOW missiles firmly planted within their launch tubes, the commander of Eagle 36 readied them for another engagement against a pair of BMPs. Just as it had been with the other Iraqi armored vehicles, these BMP-1s disintegrated under the onslaught of the two TOW missiles.

THE RECKONING

As the Bradleys and Abrams tanks of the 2d ACR were engaging and destroying the front-line elements of the 3rd *Tawakalna ala-Allah* Mechanized Division, the Iraqi unit was being pounded by coalition artillery and air strikes. These constant attacks destroyed units moving through the rear zone, disrupted command and control, and hampered Iraqi efforts to support their front-line units with artillery support: "From the time the 2nd Armored Cavalry Regiment made contact, on the night of 26 February, until the following morning when the 1st Infantry Division cleared Objective Norfolk [a critical juncture of the IPSA Pipeline Road that was heavily defended by the 3rd *Tawakalna ala-Allah* Mechanized Division and elements from at least 11 other Iraqi divisions], the Iraqi soldiers of the 18th and 37th Brigades received no respite from constant ground, artillery, and air attack" (Bourque 1997).

By 2230hrs on Tuesday, February 26, the sounds of battle died away as the 2d ACR stopped firing while the 1st Infantry Division began its "passage of lines." This complex procedure, fraught with risks even when undertaken in good visibility conditions and outside the battlespace, involved a temporary suspension of firing by the Americans:

Because the attack had stopped, the Tawakalna commander probably thought he had stopped the American advance on his left flank. Nothing, however could have been further from the truth. Just as the soldiers of the 2nd Squadron were defending against the Iraqi counter-attacks, the 1st Infantry Division began its final move towards the 73 Easting. American scouts on the forward line fired green star clusters to mark the exact passage lanes. Then, past tired 2nd US Cavalry soldiers and burning Iraqi T-72 tanks, the 1st US Infantry Division resumed the attack … Now, instead of three armored cavalry squadrons, the 18th and 37th Iraqi Armored Brigades faced six heavy battalions of American tanks

and infantry fighting vehicles and another six battalions of 155mm field artillery. The Iraqis, however, did not run. Instead, they manned their vehicles and weapons systems against the US forces. (Bourque 1997)

As this assessment indicates, the battle continued for the Republican Guard elements in the path of VII Corps' advance. In many instances bypassed by the attackers, dismounted Iraqi antitank teams and other infantry fired at the Bradleys and Abrams tanks; in several tragic instances of fratricide, five Abrams tanks and four Bradleys were destroyed by friendly fire, with six US personnel killed and a further 30 wounded.

By dawn on Wednesday, February 27, the Iraqi 18th Mechanized Brigade and 37th Armored Brigade had been destroyed; the US 1st Infantry Division controlled Objective Norfolk, and the coalition advance could continue. Elsewhere on the battlefield, the other elements of the 3rd *Tawakalna ala-Allah* Mechanized Division were engaged and destroyed by VII Corps units:

> With the destruction of the Tawakalna Division, Franks was able to focus the combat power of the 7th Corps towards the other heavy divisions of the Republican Guard Forces Command. Although part of the Medina Division would stand and fight against the 1st US Armored Division, the Iraqi high command ordered the Hammurabi Division to start moving north, across the Euphrates River and away from the American attack in the west. The Tawakalna Division's defense gave the remainder of the Iraqi Army in Kuwait the time it needed to evacuate most of its mechanized forces to Basra. (Bourque 1997)

Around 0800hrs on February 27, the 2d ACR was ordered to withdraw to the 70 Easting to reduce the possibility of further fratricide incidents occurring. On the following day, the regiment moved east and halted at the 85 Easting; a ceasefire was declared that morning. First Lieutenant Hillen sums up the 2d Squadron, 2d ACR's contribution:

> All told, and by best estimate, the squadron moved almost 200 kilometers through southern Iraq in less than 80 hours of periodic contact between the afternoon of 23 February and the evening of 26 February. The squadron destroyed more than 55 tanks and 45 other armored vehicles, an equal number of trucks, hundreds of infantry, and captured approximately 865 prisoners. (Hillen 1991: 12)

ANALYSIS

Operation *Desert Storm* finally showed the effectiveness of American-made IFVs against their Soviet counterparts. In the deserts of southern Iraq, the Bradley proved more than a match for the BMP-1 due to the American IFV's combination of superior technology, superior crew training, and superior tactics. In one notable instance, however, a BMP-1 destroyed an M2A2 Bradley during the battle of 73 Easting. Although it was a surprising upset, this BMP-1 victory had more to do with tactical timing and battlefield awareness than comparative tactics and equipment.

TECHNICAL FACTORS

While the BMP-1 itself was a rugged, durable design, its component parts were sometimes hampered by the same indifferent craftsmanship that pervaded many Soviet vehicles. After nearly a decade of combat, the 73mm gun tubes were often worn, and the Iraqi maintenance system did not stress the same level of due diligence that the Americans' did. Thus, when the ground war began, it was not surprising to see many Iraqi AFVs miss their targets, break down, or move sluggishly across the battlefield.

The BMP-1's turret suffered from a lack of ergonomics. Situational awareness in the BMP-1 was limited as the gunner was the only occupant inside the turret. Much more importantly, the BMP-1's combat optics were far inferior to the Bradley's. The Bradley could see farther than the BMP-1 and could maintain visibility even in the worst of weather conditions. In mechanized warfare, the rule is "see first, fire first, hit first" – and the winner more often than not is the one who fires first. The BMP-1's 1PN22M1 sight could only acquire targets out to 400m (440yd) at night (reduced visibility). A BMP-1 gunner could increase the visual range to 900m (985yd) with the help of an infrared searchlight, but this was still woefully less than the Bradley's visual range of more than 3,000m (3,280yd).

Although the BMP-1 carries a larger-caliber main gun, it has a much shorter effective range. The BMP-1s deployed during the Gulf War had a heavier main gun – the 73mm 2A28 Grom could (and did) disable a Bradley – but its rate of fire was lower than that of the Bradley. The BMP-1's anti-tank missiles, however, had a distinctive edge over the Bradley's TOW missiles in that the BMP-1's missiles were not wire-guided and had better handling. Both missile systems, however, had to be externally reloaded. The BMP-1 also had a lower silhouette and a higher top speed – the only unqualified advantages the vehicle had over the Bradley. However, the qualitative differences between the Bradley and the BMP-1 were only part of the equation. The real deciding factor lay in the human realm: better training, better tactics, and better motivation carried the day for the Bradley's victory in Operation *Desert Storm*.

HUMAN FACTORS

By the autumn of 1990, the US military had long since abolished the draft and transformed itself into a highly professional, all-volunteer force. American IFV crews had access to state-of-art training tools including computer-simulated gunnery programs and force-on-force maneuvers with laser sensors mounted on gun tubes. By contrast, the Iraqi Army was top-heavy and unstable following its rapid expansion during the Iran–Iraq War. Even in the Republican Guard, most of the rank-and-file Iraqi crewmen were poorly educated conscripts, and the Iraqi training programs were primitive by NATO standards.

While the Americans put their best forces forward, the Iraqi Army put its least useful conscript forces on the front lines. By the time the advancing VII Corps encountered the elite divisions of the Republican Guard, most of Saddam Hussein's combat-effective

The destroyed remains of Killer 12, an M2A2 Bradley belonging to Killer Troop, 3d Squadron, 2d ACR. Unlike Ghost 16, this Bradley was the unfortunate victim of fratricide, when an M1A1 Abrams mistakenly identified it as an Iraqi vehicle. (Tim Tomlinson)

units had been severely degraded or destroyed and most of his air force had been eliminated on the ground.

At the tactical level, the Bradley units were mobile and operating on wide frontages. In contrast, the Iraqi defenses which they encountered were hastily constructed and placed nearly all of their BMP-1s into static fighting positions. This, coupled with the BMP-1's inferior optics, defeated the purpose of having an IFV in the front-line defenses. Owing to the BMP-1's inferior optics, the Iraqi IFV would certainly be engaged before it knew the Bradley was there. Since the BMP-1s were dug into hastily built fighting positions, some of which did not allow for freedom of traversing the turret, the BMP-1 crews had to spend precious time getting their vehicles into suitable positions to return fire.

The Bradley-equipped US units also had better synchronicity with their tank counterparts. During the battle of 73 Easting, the tanks and Bradleys of Ghost Troop paired themselves into hunter-killer "viper teams" to create what was called a "see-and-shoot" combination. Since the Bradley's ISU could see farther and clearer than the M1A1 Abrams's thermal viewer, the Bradleys would spot the targets for the M1A1s so that the tanks could destroy the targets with their 120mm main guns. No such teamwork existed between the Iraqi BMP-1s and T-72s.

Finally, the Iraqis' tactical doctrine tended to place the BMP-1 strictly within the realm of infantry support. After reviewing the Iraqi Army's performance in Operation *Desert Storm*, it seems that armored reconnaissance was little more than an afterthought. Saddam Hussein's ground forces did have reconnaissance assets, but instead of using the BMP-1, the job was typically assigned to MT-LBs or to wheeled vehicles such as the BRDM-2 and BTR-60. None of these vehicles had the protection, cross-country mobility, or armaments suitable to stand up against the Bradley.

That is not to say that the Iraqis did not fight hard, but their tactics were fatally compromised by the speed and overwhelming power of their opponents:

The Tawakalna division commander, who probably perished in the battle, never had an opportunity to maneuver, use reserves, or even use his artillery with any effect. His spirited defense, however, confirmed Franks' concern that the Republican Guard did not enter the battle already defeated. They did not run away, and fought with extreme bravery. American battle reports cite the bravery of the determined Tawakalna defenders. This division had good equipment. Unfortunately, they did not know how to use it fully. For example, they did not know how to employ their equipment to ensure that they had local security, allowing the 2nd Armored Cavalry Regiment to gain contact with them without discovery. The Tawakalna division was unable, regularly, to hit the targets at which they aimed with their tanks and anti-tank guided missiles. Seldom did the Tawakalna division effectively use their artillery or air defense artillery. More important than problems in using equipment, the Tawakalna division was simply, overwhelmed. It was the application of the US Army's Airland Battle doctrine, executed by well-trained, equipped and motivated soldiers, that defeated the Iraqi forces. By dawn on 27 February 1991, the Tawakalna Mechanized Infantry Division had ceased to exist. (Bourque 1997)

AFTERMATH

The Bradley, BMP, Marder, and Warrior IFVs represented the last generation of fighting vehicles among the principal NATO and Warsaw Pact members. Notwithstanding the M1126 Stryker Infantry Carrier Vehicle or the ill-fated Future Combat System platforms, there have been no serious US attempts to develop a new IFV. Instead, the solution has been to upgrade the existing platforms every so often.

Based on lessons learned from the Gulf War, the US military developed the M2A2 ODS (Operation *Desert Storm*). The M2A2 ODS's infantry squad was increased to seven men, with the additional dismount in the position behind the turret. The major improvements included an eye-safe laser rangefinder, a built-in Precision Lightweight GPS Receiver (PLGR), and the Digital Compass Systems (DCS), a missile countermeasure device designed to defeat the normal variety of Soviet antitank missiles, and the Force XXI Battle Command Brigade and Below (FBCB2) Battlefield Command Information System. The FBCB2 was a revolutionary computer map interface that allowed vehicle commanders to see the locations of friendly vehicles via satellite. The driver received his own thermal imaging system, and the vehicle's rear stowage was further improved.

An M2A3 Bradley on maneuver. Beyond Operation *Desert Storm*, the Bradley has had a remarkable service life with the US Army, being employed in conflicts large and small – from the Balkans to Operation *Iraqi Freedom*. As of 2016, the Bradley is still in active service and military leaders anticipate that it will remain in the US Army's inventory until at least 2025. (M. Zalewski)

The US military has also developed new ammunition for the Bradley's weapons systems. Since entering mass production in 1993, the 25mm M919 round has greatly increased the first-time kill probability for any Bradley crew engaging light armor on the modern battlefield. Officially, the round is labeled "Armor-Piercing, Fin-Stabilized Discarding Sabot with Tracer," or APFSDS-T, and was introduced as a replacement for the M791 APDS-T. The projectile is made of depleted uranium and has a screw-on steel fin with tracer pellets. The round travels at 1,385m/sec (4,544ft/sec) but has greater penetration capabilities than its predecessor, and can engage targets ranging from light-armored vehicles to low-flying aircraft.

Entering service in 2000, the M2A3 featured upgrades that made the Bradley completely digital and improved the vehicle's target acquisition, fire control, navigation, and situational-awareness capabilities. Survivability of the vehicle was upgraded with a series of armor improvements (including better reactive armor) as well as an improved NBC system. Perhaps the most significant improvement found on the M2A3 was the Improved Bradley Acquisition Subsystem (IBAS) and the Commander's Independent Viewer (CIV). Both included an electro-optical/TV imaging system, and the IBAS had direct-view optics (DVO). The CIV allows the commander to scan for targets without interfering in the gunner's acquisition and engagement process. Since the dawn of the 21st century, Bradley vehicles have been equipped with the DRS Technologies Driver's Vision Enhancer (DVE), which provides a clearer digitized view of the battlefield during nighttime operations or other periods of low visibility.

Since the end of the Gulf War, the BMP-1 has had a steady, albeit reduced service life in the Iraqi Army. Following Saddam Hussein's defeat in 1991, many of the BMP-1 carcasses remained derelict on the Iraqi frontier. Although the Iraqi Army saw no major military action for the next 12 years, the remaining BMP-1s were kept in working order and were a regular sight during military parades. Nevertheless, the quality and quantity of Iraqi armored vehicles deteriorated as the 1990s drew to a close. Under the yoke of economic sanctions and war debts, the Iraqi Army and its combat effectiveness suffered.

In March 2003, at the start of Operation *Iraqi Freedom*, the remaining BMP-1s (and BMP-2s) engaged American ground forces during the highway battles on the drive to Baghdad, culminating in the famous "Thunder Run" which captured Iraq's capital city. As it had been during the Gulf War of 1991, however, these BMPs were quickly dispatched by American armor. In fact, during the intervening 12 years since Operation *Desert Storm*, the Abrams tanks and Bradley fighting vehicles had jumped a generation ahead of their 1991 counterparts – thus leaving the antiquated BMPs further behind in the technology stakes. Now American forces were arriving in-theater with the M2A3/M3A3 Bradley and its various armor, armament, and optical upgrades. Accompanying them into battle were improved versions of the M1A1 and the new M1A2 Abrams.

After the fall of Saddam Hussein's regime, the Iraqi Army was disbanded by the occupation authorities but then reconstituted in 2005. As the Iraqi Army was rebuilt under American-led authority, the remaining BMP-2s were scrapped, and contracts

A BMP-1 in current service with the new Iraqi Army. Following the 2003 US invasion of Iraq, numbers of functioning AFVs from the Saddam Hussein era were refitted and allowed to remain in service. Despite its age, the BMP-1 remains the primary IFV for the armies of Iraq, Syria, and several other countries. (US Department of Defense)

Two Iraqi BMP-1s at Tarmiya, Iraq, March 25, 2006. (US Navy)

were negotiated for new and modernized BMP-1s. These efforts led to the procurement of modernized BMP-1s from Sweden, 250 of which were sold through a Czech-based defense company known as Excalibur Army. Others came from Greece and Ukraine. Thus, despite its age and its drawbacks, the BMP-1 is likely to remain the primary IFV of the Iraqi Army for some time to come.

BIBLIOGRAPHY

Atkinson, Rick (1994). *Crusade: The Untold Story of the Persian Gulf War*. New York, NY: Mariner Books.

Bourque, Stephen A. (1997). "Correcting myths about the Persian Gulf War: the last stand of the Tawakalna," in *The Middle East Journal*, Vol. 51, No. 4, Autumn 1997.

Bourque, Stephen A. (2002). *Jayhawk! The VII Corps in the Persian Gulf War*. Washington, DC: US Army Center for Military History.

Green, Michael (2008). *War Stories of the Tankers: American Armored Combat, 1918 to Today*. Minneapolis, MN: Zenith Press.

Green, Michael, & Gladys Green (2004). *Infantry Fighting Vehicles: The M2A2 Bradleys*. Mankato, MN: Capstone Press.

Guardia, Mike (2015). *The Fires of Babylon: Eagle Troop and the Battle of 73 Easting*. Havertown, PA: Casemate Publishers.

Hillen, First Lieutenant John (1991). "2d Armored Cavalry: The Campaign to Liberate Kuwait," in *Armor*, July–August 1991: 8–12.

Macgregor, Douglas (2009). *Warrior's Rage: The Great Tank Battle of 73 Easting*. Annapolis, MD: Naval Institute Press.

McMaster, H.R. (no date). "Battle of 73 Easting." Available online at http://www.benning.army.mil/Library/content/McMasterHR%20CPT_Battleof73Easting.pdf (accessed February 5, 2016).

Scales, Robert (1993). *Certain Victory: The United States Army in the Gulf War*. Washington, DC: Office of the Chief of Staff.

US Army (2010). *War in the Persian Gulf: Operations* Desert Shield *and* Desert Storm *August 1990–March 1991*. Washington, DC: Center of Military History.

US Department of Defense (1991). *The Iraqi Army: Tactics and Organization* (Supplemental Doctrine Manual). Fort Irwin, CA: US National Training Center.

Zaloga, Steven J. (1994). *BMP Infantry Fighting Vehicle 1969–94*. London: Osprey.

Zaloga, Steven J. (1996). *M2/M3 Bradley Infantry Fighting Vehicle 1983–1995*. London: Osprey.

Zaloga, Steven J. (2009) *M1 Abrams vs. T-72 Ural: Operation Desert Storm, 1991*. Oxford: Osprey.

Zwiling, Ralph (2014). *M2A2 Bradley in Detail*. Prague: Wings and Wheels Publications.

INDEX